# building your
# academic career

# The Academic's Support Kit

*Building your Academic Career*
Rebecca Boden, Debbie Epstein and Jane Kenway

*Getting Started on Research*
Rebecca Boden, Jane Kenway and Debbie Epstein

*Writing for Publication*
Debbie Epstein, Jane Kenway and Rebecca Boden

*Teaching and Supervision*
Debbie Epstein, Rebecca Boden and Jane Kenway

*Winning and Managing Research Funding*
Jane Kenway, Rebecca Boden and Debbie Epstein

*Building Networks*
Jane Kenway, Debbie Epstein and Rebecca Boden

# building your
# academic career

Rebecca **Boden**

Debbie **Epstein**

Jane **Kenway**

**SAGE** Publications
London • Thousand Oaks • New Delhi

First published 2005

SAGE Publications Ltd
1 Oliver's Yard
55 City Road
London EC1Y 1SP

SAGE Publications Inc.
2455 Teller Road
Thousand Oaks, California 91320

SAGE Publications India Pvt Ltd
B-42, Panchsheel Enclave
Post Box 4109
New Delhi 110 017

**British Library Cataloguing in Publication data**

A catalogue record for this book is available from the British Library

ISBN 0 7619 4232 7 (Boxed set)

**Library of Congress Control Number available**

Typeset by C&M Digitals (P) Ltd, Chennai, India
Printed in Great Britain by Cromwell Press Ltd, Trowbridge, Wiltshire

# Contents

# Acknowledgements

Books such as these are, inevitably, the product of the labours, wisdom and expertise of a cast of actors that would rival that of a Hollywood epic.

Our biggest thanks go to our publishers, Sage, and especially Julia Hall and Jamilah Ahmed for unswerving enthusiastic support from the very beginning and for their careful and constructive advice throughout.

We would like to thank the authors of *Publishing in Refereed Academic Journals: A Pocket Guide* and especially Miranda Hughs for her hard work and insights which led the way conceptually.

Many people reviewed the initial proposal for the *Academic's Support Kit* at Sage's request and gave it a very supportive reception. We are grateful for their early faith in us and promise to use them as referees again!

The annotated Further Reading was excellently crafted by Penny Jane Burke, Geeta Lakshmi and Simon Robb. In addition, Elizabeth Bullen gave enormous help on issues of research funding and William Spurlin helped us unravel the complexities of US universities. All are valued friends and colleagues and we appreciate their efforts.

Much of the material in the *Kit* was 'road-tested' in sessions for our postgraduate students, colleagues and others. Many other people kindly gave their time to read and comment on drafts. We are very grateful to these human guinea pigs for their hard work and can assure our readers that, as far as we are aware, none of them was harmed in the experiment.

Chris Staff of the University of Malta devised the title the *Academic's Support Kit*, and he and Brenda Murphy provided glorious Mediterranean conditions in which to write. Malmesbury, Morwell and Gozo were splendid writing localities, although Dox 'added value' at Malmesbury with his soothing yet sonorous snoring.

We are grateful to our universities – Cardiff, Monash, South Australia and the West of England – for the material support and encouragement they gave the project.

Many people in many different universities around the world inspired the books and unwittingly provided the material for our vignettes. They are too many to mention by name and besides we have had to tell their stories under other names. We are deeply indebted to our colleagues, ex-colleagues, friends, enemies, students and past students, old lovers, past and present combatants and allies and all the managers that we have ever worked with for being such a rich source of illustration and inspiration!

We particularly thank that small and select band of people who have acted as a constant source of succour and support, wise guidance and true friendship at various crucial stages of our careers: Michael Apple, Richard Johnson, Diana Leonard, Alison Mackinnon, Fazal Rizvi, Gaby Weiner, Roger Williams and Sue Willis.

Finally, as ever, our greatest thanks go to our nearest and dearest, without whose tolerance, love and hard work these books would not be in your hands today.

R.B.
D.E.
J.K.

# Introducing the *Academic's Support Kit*

Before you really get into this book, you might like to know a bit more about the authors.

*Rebecca Boden*, from England, is professor of accounting at the University of the West of England. She did her PhD in politics immediately after graduating from her first degree (which was in history and politics). She worked as a contract researcher in a university before the shortage of academic jobs in 1980s Britain forced her into the civil service as a tax inspector. She subsequently launched herself on to the unsuspecting world of business schools as an accounting academic.

*Debbie Epstein*, a South African, is a professor in the School of Social Sciences at Cardiff University. She did her first degree in history and then worked briefly as a research assistant on the philosopher Jeremy Bentham's papers. Unable to read his handwriting, she went on to teach children in a variety of schools for seventeen years. She returned to university to start her PhD in her forties and has been an academic ever since.

*Jane Kenway*, an Australian, is professor of education at Monash University with particular responsibility for developing the field of global cultural studies in education. She was a schoolteacher and outrageous hedonist before she became an academic. But since becoming an academic she has also become a workaholic, which has done wonders for her social life, because, fortunately, all her friends are similarly inclined. Nonetheless she is interested in helping next-generation academics to be differently pleasured with regard to their work and their lives.

As you can see, we have all had chequered careers which are far from the stereotype of the lifelong academic but that are actually fairly typical. What we have all had to do is to retread ourselves, acquire new skills and learn to cope in very different environments. In our current jobs we all spend a lot of time helping and supporting people who are learning to be or developing themselves as academics. Being an accountant, Rebecca felt that there had to be a much more efficient way of helping people to get the support they need than one-to-one conversations. This book and the other five in the *Academic's Support Kit* are for all these people, and for their mentors and advisers.

We have tried to write in an accessible and friendly style. The books contain the kind of advice that we have frequently proffered our research students and colleagues, often over a cup of coffee or a meal. We suggest that you consume their contents in a similar ambience: read the whole thing through in a relaxed way first and then dip into it where and when you feel the need.

Throughout the *ASK* books we tell the stories of anonymised individuals drawn from real life to illustrate how the particular points we are making might be experienced. While you may not see a precise picture of yourself, we hope that you will be able to identify things that you have in common with one or more of our characters to help you see how you might use the book.

## Pragmatic principles/principled pragmatism

In writing these books, as in all our other work, we share a number of common perceptions and beliefs.

1. Globally, universities are reliant on public funding. Downward pressure on public expenditure means that universities' financial resources are tightly squeezed. Consequently mantras such as 'budgeting', 'cost cutting', 'accountability' and 'performance indicators' have become ubiquitous, powerful drivers of institutional behaviour and academic work.
2. As a result, universities are run as corporate enterprises selling education and research knowledge. They need 'management', which is essential to running a complex organisation such as a university, as distinct from 'managerialism' – the attempted application of 'scientific management techniques' borrowed from, though often discarded by, industry and commerce. What marks managerialism out from good management is the belief that there is a one-size-fits-all suite of management solutions that can be applied to any organisation. This can lead to a situation in which research and teaching, the *raison d'etre* of universities, take second place to managerialist fads, initiatives, strategic plans, performance

indicators and so on. Thus the management tail may wag the
university dog, with the imperatives of managerialism conflicting
with those of academics, who usually just want to research and
teach well.

3. Increasingly, universities are divided into two cultures with
conflicting sets of values. On the one hand there are managerialist
doctrines; on the other are more traditional notions of education,
scholarship and research. But these two cultures do not map
neatly on to the two job groups of 'managers' and 'academics'.
Many managers in universities hold educational and scholarly
values dear and fight for them in and beyond their institutions. By
the same token, some academics are thoroughly and unreservedly
managerialist in their approach.

4. A bit like McDonald's, higher education is a global business. Like
McDonald's branches, individual universities seem independent, but
are surprisingly uniform in their structures, employment practices
and management strategies. Academics are part of a globalised
labour force and may move from country to (better paying) country.

5. Academics' intellectual recognition comes from their academic
peers rather than their employing institutions. They are part of
wider national and international peer networks distinct from their
employing institutions and may have academic colleagues across
continents as well as nearer home. The combination of the
homogeneity of higher education and academics' own networks
make it possible for them to develop local identities and survival
strategies based on global alliances. The very fact of this globalisation
makes it possible for us to write a *Kit* that is relevant to being
an academic in many different countries, despite important local
variations.

6. In order to thrive in a tough environment academics need a range
of skills. Very often acquiring them is left to chance, made
deliberately difficult or the subject of managerialist ideology. In
this *Kit* our aim is to talk straight. We want to speak clearly about
what some people just 'know', but others struggle to find out.
Academia is a game with unwritten and written rules. We aim to
write down the unwritten rules in order to help level an uneven
playing field. The slope of the playing field favours 'developed'
countries and, within these, more experienced academics in more
prestigious institutions. Unsurprisingly, women and some ethnic
groups often suffer marginalisation.

7.  Most of the skills that academics need are common across social sciences and humanities. This reflects the standardisation of working practices that has accompanied the increasing managerialisation of universities, but also the growing (and welcome) tendency to work across old disciplinary divides. The *Academic's Support Kit* is meant for social scientists, those in the humanities and those in more applied or vocational fields such as education, health sciences, accounting, business and management.

8.  We are all too aware that most academics have a constant feeling of either drowning in work or running ahead of a fire or both. Indeed, we often share these feelings. Nevertheless, we think that there *are* ways of being an academic that are potentially less stressful and more personally rewarding. Academics need to find ways of playing the game in ethical and professional ways and winning. We do not advise you to accept unreasonable demands supinely. Instead, we are looking for strategies that help people retain their integrity, the ability to produce knowledge and teach well.

9.  University management teams are often concerned to avoid risk. This may lead to them taking over the whole notion of 'ethical behaviour' in teaching and research and subjecting it to their own rules, which are more to do with their worries than good professional academic practice. In writing these books, we have tried to emphasise that there are richer ethical and professional ways of being in the academic world: ways of being a public intellectual, accepting your responsibilities and applying those with colleagues, students and the wider community.

## And finally ...

We like the way that Colin Bundy, Principal of the School of Oriental and African Studies in London and previously Vice-Chancellor of the University of the Witwatersrand in Johannesburg, so pithily describes the differences and similarities between universities in such very different parts of the world. Interviewed for the *Times Higher Education Supplement* (27 January 2004) by John Crace, he explains:

> The difference is one of nuance. In South Africa, universities had become too much of an ivory tower and needed a reintroduction to the pressures

of the real world. In the UK, we have perhaps gone too far down the line of seeing universities as pit-stops for national economies. It's partly a response to thirty years of underfunding: universities have had to adopt the neo-utilitarian line of asserting their usefulness to justify more money. But we run the risk of losing sight of some of our other important functions. We should not just be a mirror to society, but a critical lens: we have a far more important role to play in democracy and the body politic than merely turning out graduates for the job market.

Our hope is that the *Academic's Support Kit* will help its readers develop the kind of approach exemplified by Bundy – playing in the real world but always in a principled manner.

## Books in the *Academic's Support Kit*

The *Kit* comprises six books. There is no strict order in which they should be read, but this one is probably as good as any – except that you might read *Building your Academic Career* both first and last.

*Building your Academic Career* encourages you to take a proactive approach to getting what you want out of academic work whilst being a good colleague. We discuss the advantages and disadvantages of such a career, the routes in and the various elements that shape current academic working lives. In the second half of the book we deal in considerable detail with how to write a really good CV (résumé) and how best to approach securing an academic job or promotion.

*Getting Started on Research* is for people in the earlier stages of development as a researcher. In contrast to the many books available on techniques of data collection and analysis, this volume deals with the many other practical considerations around actually doing research – such as good ways to frame research questions, how to plan research projects effectively and how to undertake the various necessary tasks.

*Writing for Publication* deals with a number of generic issues around academic writing (including intellectual property rights) and then considers writing refereed journal articles, books and book chapters in detail as well as other, less common, forms of publication for academics. The aim is to demystify the process and to help you to become a confident, competent, successful and published writer.

*Teaching and Supervision* looks at issues you may face both in teaching undergraduates and in the supervision of graduate research students. This book is not a pedagogical instruction manual – there are plenty of those around, good and bad. Rather, the focus is on presenting explanations and possible strategies designed to make your teaching and supervision work less burdensome, more rewarding (for you and your students) and manageable.

*Winning and Managing Research Funding* explains how generic university research funding mechanisms work so that you will be better equipped to navigate your way through the financial maze associated with various funding sources. The pressure to win funding to do research is felt by nearly all academics worldwide. This book details strategies that you might adopt to get your research projects funded. It also explains how to manage your research projects once they are funded.

*Building Networks* addresses perhaps the most slippery of topics, but also one of the most fundamental. Despite the frequent isolation of academic work, it is done in the context of complex, multi-layered global, national, regional and local teaching or research networks. Having good networks is key to achieving what you want in academia. This book describes the kinds of networks that you might build across a range of settings, talks about the pros and cons and gives practical guidance on networking activities.

# Who should Use this Book and How?

In our cumulative forty-five years of experience of working in higher education, the thing that strikes us above everything else is the rapid pace and direction of change in what constitutes an 'academic career'. If we were writing this book twenty years ago, it would have been a much simpler task: there were standard entry routes into the profession; standard expectations of qualifications and achievements; and a readily identifiable and largely homogeneous career trajectory. Nothing could be further from the truth now.

Environment is a key determining factor here. When C.P. Snow, an Oxford don, wrote his novel, *The Masters*, and other books about life at Oxbridge (that is, Oxford and Cambridge) colleges, he described a world shaped by a very traditional notion of collegiality, hierarchy and politics. In his university world, the fellows of the college and the values that bound them together *were* the university. There was no notion here that an academic was an employee of an institution. Rather, the college facilitated the individual's work. Similarly, David Lodge's novels such as *Changing Places* and *Small World* and Malcolm Bradbury's *The History Man* described academic life as characterised by self-governance of an organisation, nevertheless riven by petty disputes, politicking, sexual entanglements and backstabbing of various kinds.

In contrast, when Andrew Davies wrote *A Very Peculiar Practice* some years later, his imagined university was a corporate entity with managed hierarchies supplanting professional ones. While similar politicking, jealousies and disputes were depicted, nevertheless the world was a very different place. In this context, academics were employees and universities were corporations in a globalised knowledge economy.

Obviously, such works of fiction present a stereotyped view of the worst of universities of their time. However, we feel that they reasonably accurately reflect the nature of universities and how they have changed over time. The university of *Peculiar Practice* is all too familiar.

The changing nature of universities has inevitably had an impact on academic careers and individual academic identities. The changing nature of university work environments, across the globe, means that academic careers are no longer the homogeneous, stable and entirely predictable creatures that they were twenty or thirty years ago. For an individual, negotiating this minefield can be fraught with difficulties – especially when, like in *Alice in Wonderland,* the lie of the land can change almost without warning.

This book is intended to help all academics negotiate this dynamic environment to their best advantage. If this is the first book in the *Academic's Support Kit* that you are reading, then you might find it useful to read 'Introducing the *Academic's Support Kit*' before you begin. If you are reading all the books in the kit, it is probably best to read this book either first or last. You may want to read it first in order to get an overview of what an academic career entails. On the other hand, you may find it useful to turn or return to this book after you have read the others in the *Academic's Support Kit* as a way of pulling all the threads together and helping you develop a strategy for your future career.

This book will be especially useful for you if you are one of the following people:

- You may be about to begin or be at the beginning of your career in the academic world, perhaps as a postgraduate student or a newly appointed academic. You may have previously been in a different professional career such as school teaching, accountancy, the law or business.
- Because you work in a dynamic institutional environment, you may be subject to increasing pressure to develop a different academic profile and persona. For example, you may be a long-standing, senior contract researcher who wants the more secure employment that comes from having a teaching role as well as a research one. Equally, you might be someone who has done a lot of teaching but not much, if any, research. Alternatively, you might be someone who has been 'treading water' in your job and have decided to 'retread' yourself in order to get a new job at a different institution or a promotion. Finally, you may be quite dissatisfied with your lot in the world of work and have decided to take a proactive approach to making some changes.
- You might be the mentor, friend or colleague of someone in one of the above positions.

This book is about how you develop, represent and market your academic identity. Because academic work is very personalised, highly individualised and often atomised, you need to pay careful attention to how you develop and package yourself as an academic.

We've noticed that people often talk about 'being an academic' rather than being employed as one. Many people still see being an academic as a vocation and an identity rather than simply as a job. This means that work is not framed by a nine-to-five mentality and embodies a certain sense of purpose beyond earning a salary. The personal satisfaction from working in this way is often seen as compensating for the often poor material rewards that academics receive. In contradistinction, it's all too easy to let work dominate or colonise every aspect of your life to the detriment of health, well-being, family, relationships and so on.

You may want to:

- Think about where you are going in your working life.
- Reassess your career.
- Find out the best ways of presenting yourself and your achievements in order to get a job or a promotion.
- Know what the secrets of getting those plum jobs are and how to make the system work for you.
- Understand what's important in building an academic career and what isn't, so that you can be proactive in developing the aspects of your work that matter most in the career context.

The incentives to think proactively about academic careers are quite strong. Academics now work in a largely globalised labour market and this creates many more and varied opportunities than were available even a few years ago. It is also much easier to move between academia and jobs outside universities – and back again. Contemporary performance cultures mean that, for those who can demonstrate 'performance', there are plenty of opportunities available. Old disciplinary boundaries are breaking down, making it easier for individuals to transfer between disciplines as their interests and focus shifts. Moving to a new position or disciplinary area may give you better resources, treatment, promotion possibilities, access to a critical mass of people in your area and support for research. You may also be able to secure a place in a stronger research culture and intellectual environment in a university with more institutional prestige. Finally, you may acquire a nicer and better set of work colleagues. It is important to remember that a globalised academic labour market can give you as an individual a great deal of power and advantage as long as you can demonstrate that you have the right sorts of things to bring to the party.

There are also some more negative reasons why people may want a new or different job. Generally, academic positions the world over are less secure than they were and tenure (a job for life) is rapidly disappearing. This means that you as an individual must make sure that you are constantly marketable as an academic employee. Unfortunately, many universities and/or departments within them are marred by cultures of bullying and intimidation and constrained by poor resources, recognition and support. Such characteristics can generate quite strong desires to get out and go elsewhere.

Hopefully, you are quite happy with where you are, but nevertheless you will need to continue to develop your career in order to ensure that you stay happy.

First, we'd like to introduce some people who might be in the kind of position in which they would find this book particularly useful.

Gráinne became an academic after a successful career in advertising. She has been working at a university for about ten years and has just completed her PhD and is embarking on her publishing career. She is under pressure to become head of her department, but she is anxious to move to another university in her partner's home country. He is also an academic. She is unsure about how to prioritise her work activities so as to maximise her chances of achieving what she wants.

Salma was a nurse who started work at her current institution to teach in her area of professional expertise about ten years ago. Since then the university has made research activity a compulsory element in every academic's contract. At the same time it is running down the teaching in her specialist area. Salma is happy at her university and doesn't want to have to move. She also really likes teaching and thinks she might like research, but is unsure about how to make herself valuable to the institution.

▶ Inderjit is a very well qualified individual with an excellent publication record. Unfortunately, his main disciplinary area, science policy studies, is in recession and there are no jobs available to him. Because he was without an academic job he took a post as a research assistant on a professor's project in a related disciplinary area but in a business school. Whilst working in this post he used his staff privileges to study for a Masters in business strategy and was then successful in getting a permanent established post in strategic management studies.

Lucy got a first-class degree and progressed immediately to do a PhD in the same subject area and university. Following her PhD she worked as a contract researcher at the same institution and for a large charitable organisation outside higher education. She then obtained a temporary teaching job back at her *alma mater* and has recently been made a permanent employee there. She is still very young and needs to think about how to shape her future career prospects.

# 2 Why have an Academic Career?

In this chapter, we introduce the concept of the academic career as a professional one and discuss some of the pros and cons of this sort of work.

## The professional academic

An academic career is generally regarded as being a *professional* one, and therefore traditionally associated with self-regulation, expert knowledges (often mystified), high barriers to entry associated with demonstrable competence and a widely espoused emphasis on service in contrast to profitability. Thus professional work is frequently still seen as having a substantial vocational element – it is work that individuals undertake as part of their life and is a core part of their identities. Typical professions are medicine, the law and accountancy. Of course, a critical and perhaps not altogether cynical perspective on professionalism is that it enables certain groups to become powerful, influential and profitable whilst firmly established on the moral high ground.

In the majority of economies globally, during the past twenty or thirty years, the traditional notions of professionalism have been steadily undermined. Two forces have been at work here. First, neo-liberal governments and supranational organisations such as the World Bank have sought to expose professional groups to increased market pressures, creating a market for services of the same type as for cars or carrots. Expert knowledge has become a manageable commodity. This has benefited governments by cutting their own costs and stimulating the private sector. Second, market forces themselves have undermined professionalism by opening up previously restricted practices and by 'packaging' services as consumer goods. As such, professional services have become big business. These pressures have eroded the power and prestige of individual practitioners, and professional work now embodies explicit imperatives to be efficient, effective and economic – to either cost as little as possible or to maximise profitability. Simultaneously, self-regulation has been undermined and replaced with cultures of audit and performativity that are externally regulated.

For all kinds of professions, regulation has increased and autonomy and possibly work satisfaction have been reduced in recent years. Being an academic is no exception to this trend and some of what follows will reflect this.

## The pros and cons of being an academic

Here are some of the reasons why people might or might not enjoy working as an academic in a contemporary university.

### Academics are creative

Being involved in the creation of new knowledge through academic research is, for many people, an immensely pleasurable, stimulating and rewarding activity that can give a real sense of achievement and self-worth. Additionally, academic knowledge and expertise can and do have a significant beneficial impact on real people and their lives.

### Academics are paid to do what they love

Many people become academics through sheer love of their subject and excitement at being paid to study, research and teach something they thoroughly enjoy. For most academics, this is by far the most important reason for doing the job, because it is a huge privilege to be paid to do what you love doing. Academics, a bit like nurses and the clergy, are said to have a 'vocation' for their work. The down side of having a vocation is that it may legitimise low pay and poor conditions of labour. Indeed, the more ruthless managerialist universities have realised that most academics will do their work despite horrendous work pressures and poor working conditions.

One problem here is that the bits of the academic life that most of us enjoy are the research and contact with students. As universities ratchet up their demands in terms of 'productivity' and 'profitability', gaining research grants, filling in forms, meeting performance indicators and so on, those enjoyable, vocational aspects of our work are increasingly squashed so that we end up doing them (especially research), if at all, in our 'own time', but to the benefit of our employers. The impact of this can be very gendered, as those with the least 'own time' are likely to be women with caring and other domestic responsibilities greater than those of men. Not only that, it is the enjoyable but sadly marginalised activities which can and do lead to success in career terms.

## Academics have a relatively high degree of autonomy in their work

Whilst academics have less autonomy in teaching and research than they once did, this is still a significantly attractive aspect of the job. Most of us are more or less free to follow our noses, doing research that is interesting to us. While teaching is more overtly controlled than research through mechanisms such as 'quality assurance', the truth is that most of us are able to teach pretty much what and how we wish to. The reality of universities is that it is impossible to exercise constant surveillance in the lecture room and, in any case, managing academics is famously akin to herding cats.

Almost any kind of non-academic job – such as being a schoolteacher, civil servant, accountant or police officer – means having to be at your designated workplace at regular times, undertaking work which has been given you. These conditions are still a far cry from those enjoyed by academics, who, to a significant extent, arrange their own work and the times and places at which they do it.

This kind of autonomy isn't for you if you like to work in an environment structured by somebody else or who finds the responsibility of deciding what to do and when overwhelming. Not everyone has the self-motivation or discipline to be able to work well without external structures and direction. Whilst academic work does offer some opportunities to work collaboratively with others, in the main it is still largely a solitary occupation.

## Flexibility of working practices

One outcome of the autonomy enjoyed by academics is that their work patterns can be very flexible. This enables you to define the shape of your working week, within limits, and the pattern of your work across the year (or even over several years). Provided that you 'produce the goods' in terms of teaching and research output, it is unlikely that your university will seek to insist on particular times and places of work. Some institutions have tried to do this, usually with spectacularly unsuccessful results – insisting that academics work in their offices between set hours usually leads to the death of the creativity, enthusiasm and motivation necessary to doing successful research and teaching. As well as creating the right environment for good academic work, such flexibility can be very appealing to those with complicated domestic lives or people who struggle in more structured environments.

However, be warned, the flip side of flexibility is a long hours culture and a lack of good boundaries between work and the rest of life. Flexibility often leads to self-exploitation, and universities often play on this. For example, research indicates that most UK academics work well in excess of the legal maximum working week in the European Union. Because most of this work is self-controlled and is usually done at home, this exploitation goes unmarked. For those with poor boundaries, or who are susceptible to employer pressures and imperatives, the down side of flexibility can be very long hours, workaholic tendencies and severe detrimental effects on their work–life balance.

## Academic freedom

Academic freedom is highly prized internationally. Obviously this privilege is attenuated by the real-life stuff that goes on in any work place, and those who do place their trust in the right to academic freedom can and do come unstuck. Nevertheless, in principle at least, the right of academics to speak freely and critically is widely regarded as the hallmark of a good university system. For instance, in the UK, prior to 1988, academics could not be made redundant from their posts once they had tenure. In abolishing this privilege, for financial reasons, the government of the day was forced to enshrine the principle of academic freedom in law. This makes UK academics the only employee group in the country with a legally safeguarded right to speak their minds – provided that they do it in an academically rigorous way. It's important to be aware of the consequences of lack of academic freedom.

> In the 1920s and 1930s in the Soviet Union the leader, Stalin, exercised rigid control over what constituted acceptable Soviet science. This meant that scientific 'truth' was at the mercy of Communist Party cronyism. The stifling of scientific debate enabled Lysenko, a plant scientist with bizarre and unsustainable theories, to dominate agricultural policies and practices on the collective farms. As a result, many Soviet citizens went hungry.

If you're the sort of person who revels in robust debate, strenuous discussion, the challenging of orthodoxies and rigorous questioning of 'truth claims', then you are likely to enjoy being an academic and thrive in that environment. Conversely, if you are a person with very fixed belief systems in your area of interest, who hates to be questioned, then you are likely to find the academic environment quite problematic.

## Academics have a global sense of community

In most jobs, people's estimation of their own worth is usually derived from their bosses further up the food chain within their work organisation. In our experience of life outside universities, this can make working life very stressful and engender a real sense of vulnerability and conformity. For academics, the fact that they have a worldwide epistemic community of peers and friends means that they do not depend for their strokes on bosses, managers or administrators within their own institutions. While, obviously, people in positions of power and authority can and do both wield big sticks and offer large carrots, we always have an alternative – and usually more highly valued – source of recognition and affirmation. A middle manager once ruefully told an unsympathetic Rebecca that this alternative source of recognition made academics impossible to manage.

## Travelling the world and meeting people

In David Lodge's novel *Small World* his hero, Persse, is able to use his academic position to secure funding for and travel to conferences and projects in far-flung places across the globe, in pursuit of the object of his love, a woman. Whilst a slight exaggeration, it is, indeed, the case that academics who are minded to travel and who are relatively free of domestic responsibilities are usually able to go to conferences, seminars or more extensive academic visits in a range of interesting (and sometimes less interesting) places. Once there, good networkers will quickly establish a circle of useful colleagues and nice friends and acquaintances (see *Building Networks*).

The creation and dissemination of knowledge is a global activity and one that is still highly reliant upon direct personal contact. One of us once had a head of department who, entirely erroneously, thought that it was sufficient for just one member of department to attend any particular conference as they could then bring back the papers.

Most people see the ability to travel and make friends across the world as a very attractive part of the job as well as an essential one. However, some people are more parochial in their outlook and/or experience practical impediments such as acute shyness, fear of air travel, or child or other caring responsibilities. Given the importance of this sort of activity as part of your work, you really need to find effective solutions or find another career.

If you are physically disabled such that travel presents significant difficulties then you need to be both creative in finding solutions and also to enlist the support of your institution on the grounds that you have an equal right to develop your career in exactly the same way as your colleagues. Similarly, it is appropriate to make demands on conference organisers to ensure that disabled access constitutes part of their planning.

In sum, this is an important and usually enjoyable aspect of academic work. Remember, too, that many of the things that make travel difficult are transient and life does change. Things that seem impossible now, will become easier in the future and vice versa.

## An apple for Teacher

There is a great deal of pleasure to be obtained from successful teaching and the buzz that one can get from this activity has little to rival it.

There is an unfortunate tendency among some academics to be jaded and cynical about these personal rewards. To some extent, we can understand how people come to feel like this: increasing student numbers and work loads, commercial pressures and managerialist regimes of performance measurement all take the gilt off the teaching gingerbread.

If you really find engaging with other people in order to help them difficult and unattractive then this aspect of the job won't appeal to you and you are unlikely to do it well.

### Watching daytime TV

Whilst all three of us know a lot of really nice university administrators and managers, we have also all met some who seem to think that when academics aren't in front of a class of students they must be at home watching daytime television. Good academic work, whatever the discipline, must always have a large creative element. It is also frequently a solitary activity and one not amenable to the usual labour process controls. Like many forms of creativity, the hard work involved is often invisible.

This is how one senior woman academic characterised the academic labour process in a study of women's involvement in research:

I am not sure that the people who are at the real top of the university really understand how difficult it is to do all the things that we have to do. All the activities, plus try to keep a reasonable research record, it is a very difficult task. I am not sure that there is fully … I think some people do appreciate that, but I am not sure whether it is fully appreciated. It's almost as though sometimes one or two people might say – sitting at home, writing articles, books, is an easy thing to do. You could be sitting at home in front of a computer, but you might be sitting at home in front of a computer for hours and finding it really difficult. (Anna, Senior Academic)

▶

▶
(From Boden, R., Fletcher, C., Kent, J. and Tinson, J. (2004) Women in Research: Researching Women: an Institutional Case Study of Women, research and higher education, Bristol: University of the West of England)

The realities of creative academic work so well described by 'Anna' are frequently not appreciated or understood either by non-academics more widely or by some administrators within universities who have never done academic work.

# 3 Shaping up: Academic Anatomies

In this chapter, we start off by talking about the shaping of academic identities. We then go on to discuss the institutional and wider political economy contexts of academic careers. This is followed by sections in which we describe the various starting points from which people embark on academic careers and the main aspects of work that you need to think about in building your own career.

## Academic identities

Despite the relative homogeneity of universities globally, academics and their careers are remarkably heterogeneous. To some extent, and within the constraints of your abilities and the opportunities open to you, you have the possibility of shaping your own academic identity in the manner that suits you best. One of the biggest and longest-running debates in social sciences concerns the relationship between social structures and individual agency. To paraphrase from Marx (who applied the idea to men and the making of history), academics make themselves but in conditions not of their own choosing.

Unlike many other professional jobs, where you will have particular responsibilities, duties and expectations placed upon you, an academic's job is often marked by a distinct lack of specificity from the outset. The job specifications for most academic jobs, and certainly for those at the more junior levels, are really quite woolly and tend to say that the appointed person will be expected to teach, research and carry out any other duties as specified by their head of department (or other such person). Quite often, these days, there is a fourth area of expectation – that of earning consultancy fees or contributing to a professional practitioner community or policy arena.

This ability to construct your own 'portfolio' career has both advantages and disadvantages. Let's deal with the advantages first – noting that the very vagueness of most academic jobs opens up an exciting vista of opportunities for those who have the wherewithal, determination and personality traits to take advantage of them.

- In Chapter 2 we talked about the importance of relative autonomy as a key feature of academic life. One reason why autonomy survives is that job specifications tend to be minimal and academics are subject to comparatively little day-to-day direction in their work. In turn, this vagueness about the actual detailed content of the job usually leads to a significant amount of academic freedom in the choice of, for instance, research topics and strategies and even how and what to teach.
- Academic jobs tend to be specified in terms of outputs rather than how, when and where tasks will be performed. This creates the freedom to largely define your own working conditions. If you prefer to walk your dog all day and then work all night, this is broadly possible as long as you turn up for your classes and meetings on time.
- Within limits, you can create the life that you want. If you like being involved in the hurly-burly of work organisations then you can choose to do that. Alternatively, you can keep well away from most things and exist in the interstices of your university. You can even move back and forth between these two states over time. You can create the personal space necessary for good, creative work. At the same time, you can create space for your home life when and where you need it – for instance, you might need a period of gentle paddling along with your career because you have to care for a sick parent.
- As we said earlier, your sense of recognition is more likely to come from your peer epistemic community than from pleasing your 'managers'. This gives you significant control over the definition of your own criteria for success, making it easier, when you decide that you want to move on in career terms, to get the kind of profile that you need for that new job.

We'll turn, now, to the disadvantages of the ability to construct your own portfolio career.

- People who receive no, or inadequate, career mentoring and who are relatively inexperienced may find it difficult, or indeed daunting, to make major decisions about the direction of their career and the relative priorities to be attached to different activities. You may know what you want to do but be totally unable to work out how to get there.

- People who do not have a very determined sense of career direction or who are otherwise susceptible to bullying behaviours may find themselves pushed in directions that they neither enjoy nor want to pursue.
- Research indicates that women are liable to come under greater pressure than men do to devote time and energy to teaching, pastoral care of students and administration at the expense of their research.
- The system favours those with an entrepreneurial bent, prepared to elbow others out of the way as they advance up the greasy pole of the career ladder, sabotaging the ladder as they go. Whilst some people may think that competition is an effective way of enhancing staff performance, such systems tend to leave human victims in their wake and fail to maximise the potential of the entire work force, as the following story illustrates.

Mick was the dean of a large law faculty in the 1980s. Within the faculty, he distinguished between the (mostly male) researchers who had time, space and support to do their own research and the (mostly female) 'grunts', as he referred to them, who did all the teaching, administration, pastoral care and even his personal errands, like picking up his lunch and his dry-cleaning. Neither the researchers nor the so-called 'grunts' were happy in this context and he left a destructive legacy. Those who remain fall into three groups of walking wounded. First are those who, however much potential they once had, will now never become researchers and successful academics. Second, there are those who are young enough, given sufficient support, to become researchers but have a huge burden of poor self-confidence to overcome. And third, those who fought against his tyranny and have become researchers but only by being totally selfish and defending their own territory at all costs.

- It's a system that favours people who have time, energy and networking skills. Because expectations and job specifications are vague, the criteria for success are based on competition rather than an absolute standard. This norm referencing can lead to a constant ratcheting up of minimum expectations and the work rate.

Many universities now have systems for allocating work points that are specifically designed to lead to constant expansion of expected work. At the University of Fordism, the expected 'productivity' in terms of work outputs of academic staff is defined by the average of all staff outputs from the preceding year. Because the university encourages competition between staff, each faculty member strives to exceed the average from the previous year. There is also a penalty for those academics who fail to reach the average. The net result is an inexorable rise year on year of the average staff work loads and expectations to the point at which several members of staff have become ill and taken time off work for stress-related illness.

- It can be difficult to enjoy a sense of achievement when there are so few external criterion-referenced goals outside of completing a PhD. Enough is never enough and there's always something more to do that you haven't yet done. You are only as good as your last paper/book (and maybe that wasn't good enough).

The moral of this tale is that it is possible, even now, to become an agent of your own academic destiny rather than resembling the flotsam and jetsam on the changing tides of higher education. This can be achieved by hard work and having a real sense of purpose. We think that, in order to do so, you need to:

- Get the best advice possible and use it. This will often mean cultivating good friends and mentors who are more knowledgeable and experienced than you.
- Retain a clear sense of who you are and what you want to achieve as an academic. Ensure that you feel morally comfortable with your goals and targets.
- Decide what ditches you are prepared to die in and walk away from all the others if they are going to divert you from your overall goals.

- Build up a good network of professional friends. Don't be self-centred or needy in this – if you invest time and energy in helping others they are very likely to pay you back many fold.
- Pay careful attention to your personal reputation and profile at all times. It may sound pompous, but we think that a sense of satisfaction is all the sweeter if you know that you have achieved your goals whilst being a good colleague and friend.

## Career contexts

Throughout this series of books, we emphasise the strong similarities between higher education systems globally. However, national systems are marked by significant institutional diversity and also, increasingly, substantial change. It is therefore important that you correctly identify and understand the sort of system and institution that you work in and also have a keen eye as to how things are changing.

Until about twenty or thirty years ago, the image and indeed reality of universities almost everywhere was of largely independent institutions of a select or indeed elitist nature where knowledge was pursued for its own sake. Some of the knowledge produced had 'useful' commercial or other applications and university-educated people did fill valuable positions (such as being doctors), but this wasn't the *raison d'être* of the universities. University systems were paralleled in industrial economies by institutions that provided vocational education for people such as nurses, teachers and engineers. Access to universities across the world tended to be predicated on various combinations of social class, wealth, gender or ethnicity.

More recently, the interrelated phenomena of globalisation, increasing international economic competition and the notion of the 'knowledge economy' have created new demands on higher education. Thus, the production of a sizeable university-educated work force is seen as a prerequisite for effective global economic competitivity. And in the new so-called knowledge economies, the knowledge produced by universities is recast as a prized commodity. Governments now regard higher education as an important policy domain. Pressure has been exerted both to substantially expand student numbers (often within the same resources) and to shape research agendas to suit perceived socio-economic needs.

In pursuit of these objectives, higher education has been restructured in a number of countries. For instance, in Australia, the UK and New Zealand, government policy aimed at the massification of higher education has led to the translation of more vocationally oriented teaching institutions into universities. This structural change has placed an imperative on these new universities to develop their research profile as well as to maintain their teaching provision. In developing economies, the restructuring has been more complicated. For example, in South Africa the history of *apartheid* meant that institutions offering post-school education to those who were not white were severely disadvantaged in a whole range of ways. They had only poor access to money or other resources, including staff qualified to do research. Since the end of *apartheid* in 1994, the government has attempted to transform these 'historically disadvantaged universities' into institutions more like the high-status, previously white, ones and, in some cases, has amalgamated them with their more prestigious counterparts. Thus, there has been a concerted effort to improve the teaching and research capacity for the general population, necessitating wide-ranging structural change.

Structural change hasn't just been in terms of creating or merging universities and expanding their size. Less visible, but nonetheless important, changes have occurred in funding mechanisms. These have a number of aspects. Globally, government-funded higher education has been financially squeezed as business considerations of economic efficiency, profitability, throughput and generally getting 'more bang for your bucks' have taken hold. What's more, funding for research has increasingly been shifted from systems of block grants or core funding to specific short-term contracts awarded on a competitive basis. Thus few research outfits now get big slabs of long-term government money to use at their discretion. Rather, they have to find 'customers' for their research work and get them to 'buy' the research work that will be done. Those in science and technology disciplines have long argued that this restructuring has shifted the emphasis from the creation of fundamental knowledge to work that has much shorter-term applications. We think that the same trends are discernible in the social sciences, arts and humanities.

All these structural and cultural changes in university systems have engendered a great deal of heterogeneity within national systems. Thus the UK, despite a myth of homogeneity, has a range of institutions, from those which scarcely do any research and which concentrate on teaching large numbers of undergraduates with low entry qualifications to the likes of Oxford and Cambridge which retain their international reputation for excellent research and producing very well qualified graduates.

Similar patterns to this exist in many other countries. As an academic developing your career, you need to understand your local context and the exogenous pressures that shape your own environment. You won't be able to change these, but understanding them should help you to manage them better to your own advantage whilst holding true to what you think is valuable and of interest.

## Paths into academia

There are a number of entry routes into an academic career. The route you take has an impact on your likely strengths and weaknesses, probably your initial interests and how you are positioned *vis-à-vis* teaching and research.

Academics have three main types of backgrounds and we discuss each in turn.

### The traditional route

Most typically, such people do well in their first degree, taken straight from school, and proceed more or less directly to a higher research degree, perhaps taking a masters degree along the way. Their research degree acts as a form of apprenticeship for their subsequent career as academics.

Ruth went to a prestigious university and got a first-class degree in history. She got a scholarship from her university to proceed directly to a doctorate, which she completed within three years. Her first academic post proved to be unsatisfactory, so she switched to a job teaching languages (she is a good linguist) at another institution whilst continuing to research and publish in history. After a short while, she obtained a coveted lectureship in history at a reputable university, where she has since been steadily promoted.

## The professional route

As universities become more entwined with business and public services and are required to offer more vocationally oriented degrees, the crossover between academic and professional jobs is likely to increase. People entering academic careers via this route are usually hired for their professional knowledge and expertise. Their motivations may be many and varied. Some, particularly women, may feel that an academic career would fit in with their domestic responsibilities better. Others may wish to pass on their skills. They may be in professions where most work is freelance and they would welcome a regular salary, free from the pressures involved in that lifestyle. Some may just have reached a point where they want a change of direction or stimulus.

Thabi was a successful freelance journalist, who became involved in offering media training courses for academics at a local university. She decided that she would like to put her journalistic skills to use in teaching journalism and felt confident that the research she did as an investigative journalist would enable her to participate in academic research too. A job at the university would relieve her of the intense pressure of working as a freelancer.

## The teaching route

Those who come into academic work purely as teachers, and without a strong professional background, are likely to have been employed in universities without a strong research record. They may have a good first degree or a master's degree in a particular subject area and have obtained a job teaching at first or second-year undergraduate level. Such people have a very difficult mountain to climb if they are to become academics in the full sense, doing research and working in a professional capacity as well as teaching not only at undergraduate but also at postgraduate level. These people are often at the bottom of the heap in terms of status and income among university teaching staff, and will not necessarily have any security of employment (although this is changing in European countries as a result of EU employment law). Given the interest of universities in making sure that all their staff are able to contribute fully to the academic life of the institution, more systematic care is now given to the recruitment and support of people from this group.

> Giselle had done a variety of non-professional jobs, including running her own business, before going to university as a mature student. After graduation, she was unsure what to do next and accepted an invitation to do some part-time teaching as a casual employee at her university. By the time term started, she had been enlisted to lead a course at a college affiliated to the university in addition to her casual tutorial teaching. Some five years passed and Giselle acquired a substantial amount of teaching experience but remained a low-paid and marginalised member of the university staff.

Of course, these are 'ideal types' and many people are hybrids of two or more routes into the academy. A very common hybrid is for successful professionals to decide to develop themselves and their understandings of their own professions by undertaking a research degree. Sometimes, these people end up changing profession and becoming an academic in their working lives.

Whatever sort of route you have followed to become an academic, you are likely to have a distinct combination of skills and experience in the four main areas of academic work:

(1)  Research.
(2)  Teaching.
(3)  Consultancy/professional practice.
(4)  Administration.

In the section that follows this one, we deal with these four aspects in some detail. In the meantime, we set out, in Table 1, what are likely to be different people's strengths and weaknesses in these four areas, contingent on their entry route. You may find it a helpful exercise to write out for yourself what your relative strengths and weaknesses in each of these areas are. This can be an important exercise in helping you decide what is achievable and the work that you need to do.

**TABLE 1** Likely skills and competences of different types of new academics

| Entry mode | Research | Teaching | Consultancy/Professional practice | Administration |
|---|---|---|---|---|
| Traditional | You will have been well trained in research as a consequence of doing a higher research degree. You may have worked for a while as a research assistant or had some kind of postdoctoral research fellowship. The chances are that it is research that attracted you into the profession in the first place | If you've had a good induction to academia as a research student, you will have been given carefully supervised and limited teaching opportunities. However, your experience and training are likely to be quite limited. You are likely to find your early years as a teacher very challenging and time-consuming as you acquire experience and are able to bank your teaching materials | You are unlikely to have any significant work experience in a professional capacity. This can be quite a handicap, as you will not have the networks, insider knowledge or professional experience necessary for developing consultancy work. However, if you research in a practical or policy area, such connections may well develop over a period | You are very unlikely to have any extensive experience of undertaking complex administrative tasks beyond the administration of your own research project. You will be familiar with what is done in a university, for instance the setting of exams and their marking, but you are unlikely to understand the minutiae of how they happen and all the tasks involved in making them happen |
| Professional | You may be from a profession that includes elements of practitioner research as part of its professional practice, for instance medicine or teaching in schools. However, this is likely | You will probably have been employed because you have the relevant professional, technical, applied knowledge and skills for training the next generation of professionals in your field (for example nursing, | By virtue of where you have come from, you are likely to have extensive professional networks, knowledge and standing. This will stand you in good stead in gaining the kind of consultancy work that many universities | You are likely to have had quite significant experience of administration and have well-developed skills in this regard. You may have run complex organisations or projects in your professional career. Running universities may well be a cakewalk for |

*(Continued)*

**TABLE 1** *(Continued)*

| Entry mode | Research | Teaching | Consultancy/ Professional practice | Administration |
|---|---|---|---|---|
| | to be more practically and vocationally oriented, unlike academic research, which is more theoretically informed. Nevertheless, if you have this kind of background, you will not be starting academic research as a complete novice and will have some of the necessary skills and experience. You will almost certainly need to retread yourself as an academic researcher and may find this quite a daunting prospect | teaching, social work, business, chartered surveying or architecture). However, teaching undergraduate and postgraduate students in the context of a university can be quite a different undertaking. You will need to adapt both your knowledge and your teaching approaches to fit this new context | now want and the capacity and opportunity to contribute to the development of your professional area. For instance, you may sit on committees at a national level in your professional organisation | you but, sadly, universities are poorly equipped to recognise and use this significant staff resource. Hence you may become frustrated by the predominance of often less experienced professional administrators in all the positions of influence, authority and power. This won't bother you if one of the reasons you left your profession was to escape from such work |
| Teacher | If you are in this category then you probably entered higher education at a | Your primary experience will have been of teaching, probably at undergraduate level. The | You are unlikely to have significant professional experience or to be in a position to gain the | Because of your extensive involvement in teaching, you are likely to have been called upon to undertake |

*(Continued)*

**TABLE 1** *(Continued)*

| Entry mode | Research | Teaching | Consultancy/Professional practice | Administration |
|---|---|---|---|---|
| | time or in an institution where research was not a significant activity. You are unlikely to have ever engaged in higher-level research and may therefore not have any meaningful skills, experience or indeed understanding in this area. You are likely to be coming under increasing pressure from your university to start doing research or a research degree. You may view the prospect with enthusiasm, albeit finding it somewhat daunting. Alternatively, it might feel like a nightmare | quality of your teaching may be adversely affected by your lack of research experience unless you are one of the few who have assiduously maintained high levels of scholarship – that is, reading, absorbing and understanding other people's research work and ensuring that you constantly keep up to date with developing knowledge in your area | necessary professional standing in order to be able to do consultancy, professional advice work or whatever | significant administrative loads related to that teaching. You may or may not have an aptitude for it, but it goes with the teaching-only territory |

## The main elements of academic work

Universities do have to produce things and this involves, whatever type of institution they are, the organisation of the academic labour within them. Labour process theory has identified two major types of productive organisation: craft working and factory-based industrial working. In craft production systems everyone involved in the work process is skilled, to a greater or lesser degree, in every aspect of the work. In factory-based industrial working, in contrast, the production cycle is broken down into single simple stages and workers are responsible only for one stage of the process. In contrast to craft workers, factory workers need far fewer skills, command lower wages and are deemed more 'efficient' because they don't shift from task to task. Both these types of organisation are in evidence in higher education globally.

In the more traditional university the way in which work is done is more akin to craft production. Unfortunately, the increasing development of the corporate university has started a trend away from collegial craft-working knowledge production and dissemination towards more factory-like (often called Taylorised) processes.

Because it's easier to think about the labour process in car factories than in universities, we want you to imagine two different kinds of university, which we will call *Rolles University* and *Modeltee University* respectively.

*Rolles University* is a highly prestigious institution with a sound capital base, plenty of shareholder support and solid, if small, sales at the luxury end of the market. Such sales rely heavily on past reputation, and the organisation avoids any direct evaluation of current performance on the grounds that this would interfere with academic freedom. This university prides itself on producing a superlative product, whether it is research or graduates. The institution runs on traditional craft worker lines. All academic 'colleagues' must be at least fully competent in all aspects of the university's activities. That is, they must be able to research, teach and organise as well as engage in some sort of consultancy or work ▶

in support of their profession. They are expected to excel at one or more of these aspects of work but, in terms of being promoted, research is the most important criterion. Within Rolles University, there are some non-academic colleagues with administrative roles, who work in support of the academics. In this context, the university is less the employer of the academics and more the facilitator of their work. This form of craft production generally engenders a fairly healthy collegiate spirit – people tend to feel that they 'belong' and that everyone has a fairly equal work load. Because people see things all the way through from start to finish, they take pride in the job and develop a sense of loyalty, even affection, for their university. This system is made easier to implement by the fact that Rolles has a homogeneous staff as a result of its 'guild' nature – the colleagues usually recruit only people like themselves, especially to the more secure and senior positions, and the gatekeeping function is very vigorously exercised.

However, storm clouds loom on the horizon. Rolles University is now subject to increasing competitive pressures from ostensibly more efficient producers, who claim to make the same product but cheaper, better and faster. As with cars, performance and price are key criteria and Rolles is starting to look like poor value for money. What's more, the craft production process allows individual colleagues to produce idiosyncratic products, preventing the university from further developing a solid brand reputation in the market. The consequent pressure to reduce costs and standardise their output is starting to take its toll on the workers.

*Modeltee University* has only recently moved into the university sector. Having previously made bicycles, it is now attempting to make cars, so to speak. However, it perceives itself as having a strong management team, who are convinced that management is a profession in itself and a set of tools that can be successfully applied ubiquitously. Their management training has taught them to think of the university as a single, corporate venture, rather than a collection of craft worker individuals. As such, they prioritise the cost and perceived quality of the finished product over and above its method of production. Thus they have decided to Taylorise academic work, allocating individual tasks to suitable 'employees', with ruthless efficiency. Those who are good at research are tasked with research.

▶ The better teachers are responsible for the conception and development of courses, whilst barely skilled blue-collar workers are drafted in as casual teachers to 'deliver' the material to students. Any form of management or administration task of any significance is allocated to the managerial class, as it is important to maintain strict discipline and control over the labour process if efficiency is to be maximised. The employees easily become alienated and demotivated in such deskilling labour processes. It is therefore essential to maintain strict discipline over them by obliging them to demonstrate full competence in all aspects of academic work, as if they were craft workers at Rolles University. In reality, the organisation of the production process is such that it is virtually impossible to achieve this. The net result is that it is hard for academic employees to get promotion, and this keeps costs refreshingly low. In contrast, the managers at Modeltee University only have to do management work and their success in this is measured by criteria that they themselves select. Progression (as it is seen) to the management class is via a competitive process involving psychometric testing and a demonstrable commitment to Modeltee's corporate mission and vision. This mode of production has enabled Modeltee University to make rapid inroads in the market, effectively undercutting universities such as Rolles.

However, storm clouds are gathering on the horizon. Established universities such as Rolles are using their dominant market position to raise entry barriers to parvenu competitors. One way of doing this is to get the government, virtually all of whom went to a university like Rolles, to change the rules of the market. The work force is becoming increasingly disenchanted with its lot. Additionally, as conditions get worse, the university is finding it harder and harder to recruit credible employees. Finally, Modeltee has underestimated the sophistication of its customers, who are quickly coming to realise that cheapest does not mean best when it comes to universities.

Whilst these two representations are parodies, most universities encompass elements of both Rolles and Modeltee to varying degrees. Furthermore, within any one university, some departments and faculties may run like Rolles while others closely resemble Modeltee. Whichever kind of university, faculty, school or department you are in, you will occupy some designated position. With that position will come a range of expectations about the extent to which you will engage in teaching, research, administration and consultancy/professional practice. This will also vary between disciplines.

Even though you will have a place in the structure of academic production, there are many different ways of being an academic. These will be framed by the place you work, the discipline you are in and the specificities of particular posts. You have to try and match these with your own interests, talents, personal circumstances and motivations at any particular point in your life.

Be aware that some mixes of academic activities, when pursued for a long time, open up future career horizons, whilst others tend to close them down. Just remember to keep a weather eye open as to the longer-term consequences of the choices you are making now, as Marsha, in the following story, found.

Marsha had started her research career working for a major charity and had gone on from there to do contract research in a university research unit. At the same time as working as the researcher with short-term contracts on a series of other people's projects, she worked on her PhD part-time. Once she had her PhD, she started applying for permanent posts within the university sector. Although she had a good publication record and a PhD and did get interviews, she kept losing out to other people who had more teaching experience, but often less research experience. She made strenuous efforts, within her own institution, to build up her teaching experience and got herself certified by her country's professional institute for teachers in higher education. With this experience and paper qualification under her belt, she succeeded in getting a mainstream permanent academic post at another university.

We'll now look at each of the four aspects of academic work in turn.

## Research

If we understand universities to be places for the creation, critique and dissemination of knowledge, then it follows that research lies at the heart of the academic endeavour – and you can't be a core part of such a mission if you don't undertake it yourself. If you haven't already done so and you don't know how to do research, then you will find it useful to read *Getting Started on Research* before reading this section. There we deal with what academic research means and with the nuts and bolts of developing as an individual researcher. Here we are more concerned with helping you understand the career implications of the research choices you make.

Research is often thought of as an individual activity, particularly in the arts, humanities and social sciences, where the work isn't dependent on having access to expensive and often large-scale laboratory equipment. However, the opportunity and ability to do research are tied to the socio-economic conditions in different countries and the histories of the institutions in which one might work. It is, therefore, hardly surprising that across the world, universities vary considerably in their commitment to research as an activity. This will impact on you as an individual because your own opportunities and support for research will often depend on the kind of institution in which you work. You may be personally very committed and motivated to research but the presence or absence of a supportive infrastructure including things like study leave, money for conference attendance, regular research seminars, a positive attitude towards research, support in developing proposals, and so on, can have a crucial impact on what you do, when and why.

Below we offer a series of handy hints for budding researchers, which are developed in considerably more detail in *Getting Started on Research*.

### Handy hints for budding researchers

- In developing the research aspects of your career, you need to make a real name for yourself in a particular area or areas. This is what will distinguish you and make you well known, respected and regarded. This means that you have to stake a claim on your own territory that will be yours to pan for gold in. You must develop your own distinctive area(s) of research, making sure that the different aspects of your work hang together in a way that you can justify (to yourself and others) as a coherent personal intellectual project. It will do you no good in career terms if your work is a disparate ragbag of bits that looks incoherent and has nothing distinctive about it. Don't just follow trends in research, help to set them if you can.

- The research process constitutes a number of different sorts of work activity. It may include: developing your own projects; getting funding; data collection and analysis; managing resources; writing; disseminating; and networking. In order to demonstrate that you are a competent researcher, you will need to be at least proficient in all aspects of research work. You must be proactive in identifying aspects of the research process where you need to gain experience, expertise and a reputation and taking the appropriate action. You will find help with what to do about these various aspects in *Getting Started on Research, Winning and Managing Research Funding* and *Writing for Publication*.

- You need to be proactive and strategic in picking people to work with. Working with more senior and famous colleagues can help to boost your own reputation and get your name known quickly. However, it is treacherously easy, when you are relatively inexperienced, to be pushed or seduced into working on projects that really don't interest you, if people head them up whom you admire or wish to be associated with. You also need to be wary of being known only as a famous person's '*et al.*' – don't be a lifelong sidekick. Second, if you work with people from other disciplines, they can widen your experience and research expertise (and you theirs) and you can develop your reputation across a number of disciplines. Third, successful research collaborations can be fruitful in developing the general networks to which you belong and in opening up particular opportunities for interesting research or even jobs in the future.

- Your name on things is an important part of building your research reputation and career. Make sure that you get appropriate recognition for research outputs such as books, chapters, journal articles, reports, videos, etc. We give further advice on authorship in *Writing for Publication*. Similarly, when you conceive of and design a project, you need to ensure that you get the credit for it and are named as the principal researcher or, at the very least, as an equal co-researcher. If funding bids are being submitted and it really is your project, then make sure that the documentation reflects this.

- Make sure that your publishing supports the development of your profile. When you publish, think about the audience you want to speak to and choose journals that both suit your work and are read by people who have an interest and influence in your chosen field. You need to be and look credible within your chosen field, and this means making strategic choices. When you work in a cross-disciplinary team, you need to ensure that every member of the team is able to gain publication in places appropriate to her/his field.

- While you are likely to have some projects over a career to which you are more committed than others, getting yourself involved in research that you don't find interesting is a recipe for disaster. At the same time, you will need to be adaptive, finding ways to fit your interests to what can be supported and, if necessary, funded. As you develop an established reputation for research and become more senior, you may also wish to support less experienced colleagues by participating in their projects at their request. Whatever your position, you need to be aware of the research environment and the demands of your own government, region and university.

- And finally, if you want advancement in your career, make sure that your research works for you in terms of developing your profile and establishing the necessary networks of contacts that will be essential in getting promoted or getting a new job. This includes going to the right conferences, schmoozing (but not sucking up to) the right people, joining the right project teams and publishing in the right places. Don't overdo it, or you will get up everybody's nose. More help can be found in *Building Networks*.

## Teaching

The overwhelming majority of universities earn their bread-and-butter income by teaching students and this is, therefore, a core work activity for most academics. Despite its often compulsory nature, the good news is that teaching work is frequently enjoyable and something from which you can derive a great deal of personal satisfaction.

As universities become increasingly commodified and students are asked to pay increasing amounts for their own education, so teaching has come to be seen as a commercial transaction in which consumers (students) buy knowledge from producers – or maybe retailers (teachers). This recasts traditional pedagogical relationships as one of service providers and consumers. Our own feeling is that the student/consumer is not empowered by this process and that the best teaching and learning come when the relationship is based on mutual respect and trust rather than evaluations of 'value for money' and 'service quality'. This recasting of pedagogy as a straightforward commercial exchange (fees for knowledge) fails to recognise the importance of challenging students, making them work hard and the transformative effects of good education. If the 'customer is always right', and what the student/customer wants is merely to pass exams, then they will not learn much of value, but only how to pass exams. Managerialist universities like Modeltee, however, want academics to treat students/customers as if they were always right, ensuring that they pass exams however little work they do, in order to keep them happy. If you, as an academic, cave in to such pressures, then you will not only be selling the students short but will also become a disillusioned and bitter teacher, unable to enjoy the processes of creating and sharing knowledge with students. In our experience, even students who ask, 'What do I need to know to pass the exam?' can be successfully challenged and become engaged and enthusiastic learners.

Because teaching is so central to the finances and missions of universities, it tends to be the most closely directed aspect of our work. At the most basic level, for instance, our students have to pass assessments that are formally governed by university regulations. This control may encourage some academics to abrogate their sense of professionalism, potentially inducing a passive conformity that can in turn lead to resentment and loathing of teaching itself and, even worse, of students. The one thing we would seek to impress on you about teaching is that it doesn't have to be like that. If you can develop a positive approach to teaching, where you feel able, equipped and confident to deploy your professional skills in tackling the work, then you will enjoy it more and the students will gain more from you. If you have to be involved in teaching, don't start out with the idea that it is simply unavoidable drudgery. Rather, approach it as something that both you and the students can really enjoy and learn from.

1. *Be prepared – but not too prepared.* A general rule is that each hour of class contact is really three hours of work for the teacher. You can't teach well unless you are well prepared. However, people who are inexperienced or unconfident tend to go overboard on preparation. If you are in the very early stages of a teaching career or developing new teaching you will find the going much tougher than your more experienced colleagues. What you need to do is to develop a bank of routines, resources, activities and material that you can quickly and efficiently draw on whatever you are called on to teach. Always remember that, especially with undergraduate teaching, it is highly unlikely that anyone in the class knows more than you. If you get asked about something you don't know about you can suggest that the whole class (including you) finds out about it before you next meet. You are a learning facilitator, not the fount of all knowledge and you shouldn't be ashamed to say so.

2. *Keep your boundaries.* Whilst you shouldn't approach teaching as an unavoidable chore, neither should you let it take over your working life to the exclusion of all the other stuff that you should be doing. This can all too easily happen: teaching is often formally timetabled and therefore becomes the clock by which all life is regulated. Moreover, because it is more tangible and defined as a process than research it can look like a safe haven where you want to shelter away from all the other things that seem more onerous. Students can be very demanding and 'needy'. Whilst they may need your help, you shouldn't let them dictate what form it takes. For instance, if they have missed a class because of a hangover and come to see you for a personal tutorial to catch up, it is better for both of you to send them away with a reading list than to devote your precious time to compensating for their shortcomings. You can do very practical things to keep good boundaries: for instance, make sure that students make appointments in advance to see you and specify how much time you will give them. This will ensure that they come and see you only when they really need to and that they prepare themselves properly to make best use of their slot. If you might be tempted to let students gobble up your time or find it socially difficult to get them out of your office then it might be best to hardwire-in time constraints – such as having another student waiting in the corridor or a meeting to go to. We wish we could be

like the Queen of England, who reputedly ends personal audiences by tinkling a small bell on a shelf under the table, summoning someone to take the visitor away!

Being a teacher often involves some aspects of pastoral care. However, you should recognise your limitations in terms of time and skills. If students need a doctor or a therapist, suggest they go to one. Most universities have such services available. You can't add parent/counsellor/doctor/financial adviser to your list of jobs.

3.  *Develop a portfolio of teaching experience.* Inevitably, when you are new to teaching, you will be asked to undertake relatively straightforward teaching tasks. As time passes, you must make sure that you accumulate experience of different levels of teaching such that you can demonstrate your competence across the range from undergraduate to taught postgraduate to research supervision. Don't over-stretch yourself and don't be afraid to drop some activities as you undertake increasingly sophisticated teaching tasks.

4.  *Make your mark.* It's good to get involved in teaching innovations but don't get involved in every new fad and fancy. Appropriate amounts of such work will give you a better return in terms of job satisfaction and will provide rich material for your CV or résumé.

5.  *Maintain your interest.* Like any regular meal, most degree programmes (especially at undergraduate level) include the staple core elements (mashed potato or Sociology I) and some choices to suit individual tastes (stewed rabbit or the Sociology of Sexuality). In cooking and teaching it's only fair that everyone mashes some potatoes from time to time as well as getting an opportunity to strut their stuff on the fancy things that they enjoy. You will have to teach on core courses of some kind, but don't let your department or school dump these on you in the long term or as your only teaching. You can enjoy the challenge of teaching core courses, but you will also want to blend aspects of your own specialist research interests into what you teach, giving the students the benefit of your specialist expertise. In addition, teaching a specialist course in an area relatively new to you can be a great way of further developing your own research expertise.

6.  *Get a good enough reputation.* In career terms you need to be known as at least a competent and conscientious teacher. As long as you know your stuff reasonably well, prepare adequately, respect your students by turning up on time and doing what you promise to and conform to the bureaucratic requirements placed on

teachers (such as marking exams on time), then it is quite hard to get a bad reputation. It follows that if you have an outstanding aptitude for teaching and/or it is something that you want and are able to devote a lot of energy to, then you can become a really good teacher. In our experience however, superlative researchers and good-enough teachers are invariably promoted over superlative teachers and good-enough researchers.

7. *Be up to scratch*. Most universities now implement some sort of regime of student evaluation questionnaires – evaluation of you by your students, that is. Sometimes these are just lip service to 'customer satisfaction' but in a number of countries they are of increasing importance. In the USA for instance, such questionnaires may be used to determine salary levels. In the UK, the government plans to make student evaluations of individual courses available nationally on-line to 'facilitate student [whoops, customer] choice'. It may therefore be the case that you have to take such evaluations very seriously if your career is to develop. You can't do a lot about such systems, especially if they are beyond your control, except be a good teacher. Additionally, you could collect your own feedback using more pertinent questions and methods of engaging with students' opinions.

    Some universities also have formal schemes for peer-led or management evaluations of the 'quality' of your teaching. This might typically involve someone sitting and watching you do a lecture once a year. We are sceptical of the value of many such schemes. If you are subject to them, then you need to find a way of performing well whilst minimising how much time and effort you put into the process.

8. *Ticket to teach*. It has been traditionally assumed that, if you get an academic job, you can teach. This is not necessarily the case, and most academics find the process of learning how to teach quite difficult. If you are in an institution where there is no formal support in teaching you how to teach, then you need to seek out experienced colleagues who can help you. In some systems university teachers are increasingly obliged to undertake formal teacher training, perhaps leading to a qualification. It is by no means the case that such formal courses are always better than the more traditional forms of informal support, but they do look good to external validation bodies. If your formal support isn't good, then you will still have to find your own help. Whatever, if your

system really requires you to have a formal qualification then you will need to just get on and do it.

9. *Getting a manageable work load.* If you are relatively junior, you may feel, or indeed be, overburdened with teaching duties. If at all possible, you should find ways of keeping your teaching duties under control. Whilst individual schools or departments are increasingly less able to limit total student numbers, you can make collective decisions on matters such as student contact hours. Additionally, you and your colleagues should always seek to ensure that work is equitably (which isn't the same as equally) distributed.

## Consultancy and professional practice

Academics have always played their parts in public affairs and, as appropriate, in offering advice to governments, working with and for industries, taking part in relevant professional activities and so on. This is a traditional part of the job and can be invaluable in helping you build networks, providing you with access to research sites, allowing you to use your expertise to disseminate your work widely and even to influence how things are done in practical settings. However, with the corporatisation and marketisation of universities, academics are increasingly expected to actively seek this work out. In the UK, it has become known as the 'Third Mission' of universities (the first two being research, that is knowledge creation, and teaching, that is knowledge transmission).

There are a number of problems in this for academics. First, it may be that the knowledge you want to produce and disseminate does not fit neatly into narrowly profitable objectives. Second, even where what you want to do is 'useful' to people in the outside world, they often don't want to pay for your work. After all, they have already paid their taxes and why should they pay again for your labour?

If you are a full-time employee of a university, then it will have to pay for your labour whether you are doing consultancy work or not. This means that the marginal cost to the university of your time being spent on consultancy or professional practice is confined to any cost associated with replacing your teaching. Anything earned by you for the university over and above that is a welcome surplus to an often cash-strapped institution. Additionally, some universities want you to bring in this extra money as well as carrying a full teaching and research load.

That way the university gets the kudos of having its employees performing consultative and professional services and the real cost is born by the academics who must do the extra work.

Because competition for such work can be quite brisk, and because the contracting organisation usually feels that public universities should do the work for next to nothing, the costings of such contracts often underestimate the amount of work really involved – as Bruce's story below shows.

> Bruce is a career contract researcher in a unit where the staff have not only to cover their own salaries with the research contracts they win, but also to make a net financial contribution to the central university. There is plenty of work available to tender for, but also plenty of other universities vying to do it. This means that price is a key consideration in winning funding. Salaries are fixed by national agreement, so the only way to bring the cost of a contract down is to underestimate the number of person days the work will take to do. Typically, on a job which takes, say, twenty-five days, the unit will bid for just twenty days of Bruce's time. This means that every month, Bruce has to do twenty-five days' work in just twenty working days. Consequently, he works late and at weekends even though he has a young family. He also has no time to turn the consultancy reports that he produces into peer-reviewed academic papers and this means that he cannot build up the research record and profile that he needs to move on in his career and that he deserves in the light of the work that he does.

In sum, you need to use your opportunities for consultative and professional work well, without allowing them to use you and take away from your research and teaching activities. Such matters are dealt with in detail in *Winning and Managing Research Funding*.

### Handy hints for consultancy and professional practice

1. *Use consultancy for your research.* Consultancy and work in a professional capacity can be good for your research in certain disciplines and fields of study. If chosen well, such work can give

you access to information, informants and research locations that might otherwise be hard for you to find. It can also help you build your profile within and beyond the academic world. On the other hand, these activities can become a time-consuming distraction that prevents you from paying proper attention to the main parts of your job – research and teaching. So be selective.

2.  *Choose well.* Doing extensive consultancy/professional work can act as a kind of sink down which you pour endless amounts of work but all that happens is that it disappears into a black hole and can therefore often do little to enhance your academic reputation. For instance, in much of this work the intellectual property rights (see *Writing for Publication*) over the research belong to the contracting organisation. This may mean that you are prevented from publishing your work in journals or books or even presenting it at conferences. Equally, the extensive and sterling (usually unpaid) work that you do serving on all kinds of professional committees may count for little or nothing in job and promotion applications if your research record has suffered as a result. Again, be selective in what you do, when and why. Choose those pieces of work that are both manageable and useful to you for your own purposes.

3.  *Take control.* If you have come into the academy from a profession, you may well want to continue to contribute to it through consultancy and professional work. This is entirely laudable. However, you now have a different career in which this kind of work can properly form only a relatively minor part of your whole working life. So you need to keep things in perspective and keep control over the amount that you do.

4.  *Develop 'user group' networks.* If you are applying for research funding, it is often the case that the funders require references from 'user groups' – that is, people in the public, private or voluntary sectors who may well want to make use of your findings in their work. You will, undoubtedly, meet such people in your consultancy and professional work and will be able to utilise these networks in your funding applications.

5.  *Making a wider contribution.* Doing consultancy can be an important way of making a contribution to the wider society and of disseminating your research beyond the academy. In deciding which consultancies to accept or seek, you need to think about what its overall contribution will be, both to your own work and to the community more generally.

## Administration

'Administration' is a vague and amorphous term and requires some definition. Academic work has always involved a certain amount of basic organisational stuff for students (such as registering them or compiling lists of examination results) and for research (such as hiring research staff or administering research budgets). There has also always been a certain amount of work to be done around forward planning for teaching and research, critically self-evaluating the university's activities, ensuring staff continuity, proper budgeting, governance and accountability. Contributing to such work is part and parcel of being a good university citizen.

Such organisational work used to be called administration and was usually the domain of academics supported by career administrators, many of whom were really excellent at their jobs. The proper and efficient execution of such work is vital to the function of the university.

However, with the corporatisation of universities came the conviction that universities could be made more efficient and businesslike if they were 'better organised'. This engendered a process whereby straightforward administrative, organisational tasks were reified and then deified as 'management procedures'. This inevitably involved them becoming much more complicated in order to justify their new, enhanced status. This new management work necessitated an increase in the number of administrators to do the extra work and the creation of a cadre of managers specially qualified to manage the whole process. In order to pay for this new management work, resources for academic work were reduced. Academics were persuaded of the merits of this on the basis that their jobs would be much easier if professionals did all the administration for them.

In fact, what has happened in many instances is that management procedures consist of demanding and requiring academics to respond to management requests. For instance, as part of good professional practice, conscientious academics have always sought the views of their students on the courses that they had taught. This work would be done with the support of their secretaries. Now, at many institutions such 'quality assurance' work has become a management responsibility and the academics have lost their secretarial support because the resources were needed to appoint a Quality Assurance Manager. The Quality Assurance Manager now issues instructions to academics about how to conduct student evaluations and demands reports from them. Thus academics are responsible for more work than they did before, but have no secretarial support to assist them. However, they can at least be assured that they are now better managed and quality assured.

In sum, then, straightforward administrative work has now been largely taken away from academics, made more complex and turned into 'management'. What's more, academics have a net workload gain because they now have to respond to management demands. Once the management machine has been created, it has to keep doing things in order to justify its existence. Accountants should consider the costs of all this: the cost of managers' salaries and the opportunity costs of academics' time. If you think that we're over-egging the pudding here, consider the following, absolutely true, story.

In 1993 Dimitrios, a lecturer at Rolles University, wanted to go on study leave from his department. He chatted to his head of department in the corridor, who agreed that he had worked for long enough to warrant it and that the department could cope during his absence. The head of department wrote to the university registrar, who, as a matter of formality, sent a standard letter out to the head of department and Dimitrios, agreeing to the leave.

By 2003 Dimitrios (partly as a result of a very successful study leave) was a professor at Modeltee University. The dean sent out a four-page letter and form that he had composed asking people if they wished to apply for study leave. Dimitrios spent a very full day writing his application and submitting it to the research manager by the designated date. A committee consisting of the dean and two other professors were then sent all the applications and subsequently met to discuss them. This stage of the process took about a day's work for each of these three people. The dean then wrote to the successful candidates, including Dimitrios, informing them that their request had been granted and composed a lengthy annual 'Research Review' report for circulation to the university authorities and all staff in the faculty in which the process by which the study leave had been decided was described and the results were announced. Many of the hundred or so staff spent time wading through this lengthy report because they wanted to know who had got study leave.

▶ A few weeks before Dimitrios's study leave was due to start, the assistant dean sent around an email to everyone setting out, at some length, the procedures to be followed and the forms to be filled in if a staff member wanted to be absent from the university during term time. The same manager then sent Dimitrios's head of school a blank form for those requesting permission to be absent during term time, asking her to ensure that Dimitrios completed it, that she countersign it and that it then be returned to the assistant dean for him to countersign also. Dimitrios's head of department forwarded this to him in a spirit of despondent exasperation. Dimitrios completed the form, explaining ironically in the section that asked for an explanation of why he wanted the dean's permission to be absent during term time that he wished to take up the faculty's offer of study leave. That is, he wished to request permission to go on the study leave that the dean had given him permission to go on. As a final act of defiance, he asked for a copy of the form as counter-signed by the assistant dean to be returned to him 'for his files'. He then passed the form to his head of department, who in turn signed it and passed it to the assistant dean for signature. He signed it and a secretary took a copy of it to send to Dimitrios and placed the original in his staff file.

Just two weeks before the start of his study leave Dimitrios received a second, three-part carbonated form for him to sign. This was a university form that needed to be completed by a member of staff going on study leave, countersigned by the dean and then finally signed by the deputy vice-chancellor. Dimitrios completed this form and sent it to the dean's secretary, who presented it to the dean. He countersigned it and the secretary sent it to the deputy vice-chancellor's secretary. She put it in his folder for signature, and eventually he signed it and sent it back to her. She separated the three parts, put one copy on the deputy vice-chancellor's file, sent one to the dean and sent the third copy to Dimitrios, who, by this time, was abroad on study leave.

You may like to spend a few minutes thinking about how much money Modeltee spent going through this farce and to what, if any, benefit. The cost of replacing Dimitrios's teaching (the only real cost) was about 8 per cent of the annual cost of employing him.

Whilst there is real and important work to be done around the administration of teaching and research, you must be able to correctly identify the management 'froth' of a lot of these tasks. For instance, it is crucial that examination results are accurately and promptly reported back to the university and such work must always be approached by academics with diligence and professional standards. In contrast, if you are asked to produce a three-page critical self-evaluation of your course at the same time, in which you must reflect on your own shortcomings, so that this document can be filed in the right box, on the right shelf and then forgotten, you can afford either not to do it or, if forced to, to do it with the diligence that it deserves. If you spend your time responding endlessly to management demands that were created only to justify the existence of management in the first place, you will never have the time and energy for a proper academic career.

That said, here are some handy hints for keeping the Management Hydra under control.

## Handy hints for reluctant administrators

1. *Take on manageable tasks.* You do need to be able to demonstrate that you are capable of competently contributing to the administration work of your university at an appropriate level. You should take on administrative tasks that are manageable, that you genuinely think need doing and that look good on your CV – for example, convening a course or acting as examinations officer. It looks even better on your CV if you can get this job called 'Director' of something or other (but not the stationery cupboard).

2. *Choose jobs that allow autonomy.* Try to find tasks that are discrete and allow you a reasonable degree of autonomy. In particular, you don't want to be doing a job where you end up constantly referring and deferring to someone in the central administration of your university. Being responsible for teaching 'quality' compliance is an example of a particularly onerous task with no autonomy, no need to understand what quality in teaching is, constant deference to external bodies and management systems, little or no reward, constant flak from your colleagues, who hate it, and no real point. If you have to be on a committee, it's better if you can chair it (provided you have learnt how to minimise the time

spent in meetings and the work that you and other people carry away from them).

3.  *Look after your administrative profile.* Make sure that you develop your administrative profile in the same way as you do your teaching. You'll need to be able to demonstrate that you can do a range of tasks, for instance chairing committees, managing budgets and so on. If necessary, discuss with your head of department what it is you need to do (or learn to do) and how you may gain that particular experience.

4.  *Don't be the token minority all the time.* If you are in some kind of 'minority' category (for example, have a disability, or are a woman, or are from an ethnic minority) then there is a tendency for universities to call on you often where representation of your minority is required. If you are a senior woman, it is likely that you will, for example, be asked to serve on huge numbers of appointment panels because equal opportunities policies usually specify that all such panels must include at least one woman and there are relatively few women in senior posts in universities. While it is certainly important that women are on appointment panels, it's not your personal responsibility to make up for the shortcomings of previous appointments policies at the expense of your own career development. You need to decide in advance how much of such work it is reasonable for you to do and stick to that.

## Balancing acts

We've outlined the four main types of activity which you may undertake in varying proportions during your career. The pressures on academics can be such that it feels that you are being asked to do 'a lot of this, more of that, all of the other, and do it by tomorrow, today and yesterday'. You need to get the balance between these activities right for you, and this will involve careful negotiation over your workload mix with your university. Some universities have ideal proportions – say 40 per cent teaching, 40 per cent research and consultancy, 20 per cent administration. Yet others attempt to precisely demarcate the hours over the year to be devoted to particular tasks. These detailed systems are often a fool's errand because of the ill defined nature of much of the work to be done. However, you can use them to your advantage. For instance, if you are asked to do some administrative work that is not genuinely important, you could apologetically explain that, whilst you are keen to do the work, you have already exceeded your designated admin working hours and unfortunately have no time to do it. If you are asked to take on something new, the bargain must include dropping an equivalent quantity of work. For example, if you are going to take on a new master's course, you may need to drop some undergraduate teaching.

Ultimately, it is crucial to get the balance right for you, which means a mix of work that will let you achieve your career aims.

## Reputation matters

You have to think of yourself and your career as a package; the wrapping on the package is your reputation. It is easier for people to see the package than to see the person inside. You need to pay serious attention to building your reputation in all aspects of your work and to be conscious of the fact that the global university community is, in fact, a very small village.

### Infamy! Infamy! They've all got it in for me! Handy hints on keeping a good reputation

1. *Look after your all-round reputation.* The most important aspect of your reputation is the name you make for yourself as a researcher, as a teacher and as a good colleague. You must safeguard your reputation in all aspects of your particular workload mix. Don't get known, for example, as someone who produces brilliant research publications at the expense of woefully neglecting students' needs.
2. *Don't use academic critique to express personal malice.* Sometimes people express personal antipathies as academic critique. Don't do this yourself and learn to recognise such behaviour for what it is when you are on the receiving end.
3. *Be careful about gossip.* Be sensitive to the personal networks around you. We all enjoy a good gossip or a spot of bitching. Be careful who you do it with and never, ever, *ever* do it in writing or on email.

4. *Be a good colleague.* It's always best to be the best possible colleague that you can, even if you sometimes have to do it with gritted teeth. News about how you treat your colleagues travels, and lack of consideration for them will rebound on you. Be forgiving and gracious and always be ready to apologise if necessary to repair damaged solidarities.

5. *Don't mix sex and work.* Mixing sex and work is fraught with danger. Needless to say, the last thing you need is a reputation for sleeping with students, your colleagues' partners or people you manage at work.

6. *Don't be inappropriately sexual.* And finally, a note on sexuality at work – that is, the ways in which all of us may use our bodies, our seductiveness (wherever that comes from), our appearance and clothing and our sexiness in our work relations. Especially for academics, intellects and ideas can be incredibly sexy and seductive – which is nice. What is not nice is using this sort of sexuality as a means of getting your own way, feathering your own nest or doing colleagues over. So don't dress to kill (whether you're male or female), flirt or otherwise be inappropriately sexual at work. You may think it will get you places, but it will also undermine your reputation as an academic who should be taken seriously.

# 4 Presenting Yourself: *Vita* Statistics

In this chapter we deal exclusively with your *curriculum vitae* or, if you prefer, your résumé (these are the same thing).

## Why is it so important?

We're going to devote a whole chapter to CVs (as we shall call them) because this is the single most important document that you will ever compile relating to your career development. You need to approach the compilation and maintenance of a CV as an on-going, career-long task.

If you haven't already got one in a good state you need to make a start now. Do not underestimate the amount of time and effort that this work will take. Remember that your CV needs to be accurate and truthful. A prospective employer may need to verify your statements regarding, for example, work permit status, qualifications and may need to take a criminal record check (especially if the job involves working with children). False statements made in job applications may invalidate any subsequent appointment. Don't risk it. Having said that, our aim here is to help you present yourself in the best possible way.

## CV FAQs

### What is a CV?

*Curriculum vitae* is a Latin term that means, literally, 'the course of a life'. In practice, it is a document that sets out a whole host of your personal details, experience and achievements as they relate to your working life. Your full CV should be a well set out, up-to-date, thoroughly accurate and exhaustive data bank of all of these details, although you may well shape slightly different versions of your CV for different purposes.

## Why do I need one?

You need a good CV when applying for jobs, seeking promotion and trying to get research funding. In addition, you will need to draw information from your CV for things such as when you're asked to be an external examiner for a course or a research thesis; for audits of teaching and research activity; if your faculty or department has to be validated by an external professional body – in short, any circumstances in which somebody needs to judge your individual professional competence or that of you and your colleagues collectively.

Compiling your CV also provides you with a crucially important opportunity to reflect on and plan further developments in your career. What's more, for those moments of self-doubt about just how good you are, a well set out CV that demonstrates real achievements can be very reassuring (and contrariwise, it might make you buck your ideas up and get on with things).

When reflecting on your CV and how you need to develop it, think about whether it is what Rebecca's PhD supervisor called a 'staying' or a 'leaving' CV. A 'staying CV' is that of the good university citizen, including plenty of committee work and administration, pastoral care of students, a heavy teaching load as well as a credible research record. A 'leaving CV' will reflect the interests of a prospective new employer and will probably highlight research achievements, while still showing that you are generally competent and willing across the range of duties undertaken by academics. You should never place yourself in the position where your CV won't allow you to leave.

We introduced Gráinne in Chapter 1. Her university would very much like her to become head of department, a job that she could undoubtedly do extremely well. It would not only bring an attractive financial stipend with it, but would also allow her to make a real contribution to the well-being of her colleagues and students by improving significantly the management of her department. But Gráinne has recently completed her PhD and has just begun to build up

▶

▶ her publications record. She would like to move to another university, possibly in another country; her field is highly competitive in research terms and she would not get the kind of job she wants without a substantially better list of publications. She has therefore decided to turn down the opportunity to be head of department and concentrate on lengthening her list of publications.

Gráinne is planning well ahead. However, planning to move is not the only reason why you need a leaving CV. Always remember that your current circumstances may change rapidly and without much warning – you might get an obnoxious new dean who makes your life a misery, or you might be made redundant. Never, ever thoroughly nail your colours to a single university mast – the ship might sink at any moment. Also remember that you don't necessarily know when your perfect, dream job is going to come up. If you have a staying CV when it does, then you won't be in the best possible position to grab it.

## When do I need to do it?

It follows from what we've said above that, because a CV is an important career planning tool and you may need one in a hurry when that perfect job comes up, it is never too early to put your CV together. Don't be put off starting because you have comparatively little to put in it. Starting now will encourage good work practices, help you establish a good basic framework and ensure that all your on-going work activities are recorded and not forgotten.

## How do I get and keep my CV in good shape?

Preparing and maintaining your CV has to be a collaborative, interactive and iterative process. You need to enlist the help of your friends, family, mentors and more experienced colleagues because it is a rare gift to be able to see ourselves as others see us.

Later in this chapter we set out what we think is a pretty good CV pro-forma that you might like to use as the basic framework for your own. Using a framework helps to structure your recollections and thinking. Most people find constructing a CV using this type of framework quite an affirming experience – they start off thinking they've achieved very little or nothing but as they start to fill in the boxes they find that they've actually done quite a lot.

You should show your draft CV to people who know you and/or who know what an academic CV should look like and ask for feedback. Typically, they will remind you of things you've done or skills you have demonstrated that you have overlooked or underplayed. They will also help you with layout, prioritisation and emphasis. This can be a fairly lengthy iterative process. Once you have done this basic spadework, keeping your CV up to date should be relatively easy and a far less time-consuming task.

You must update your CV regularly, and little and often is best. Some people pop things into their CVs as soon as they occur – for example, a paper accepted for publication. Others keep a running note, perhaps in the back of their diary or a list on their notice board, of things to add. Yet others update it with great regularity on the same day each month and set up their computer to prompt them to do this. You need to adopt a system that works for you. Whatever your system, you must:

- Have a system whereby details that need to be included on your CV do not get lost or forgotten – something that can happen all too often.
- Regularly revise your CV to reflect major new developments in your work. For instance, you might move into a distinctly new theoretical area.
- Revise your CV for current accuracy. For instance, you might have put down a project that you were seeking funding for and it has not come to fruition or has petered out. Equally, you might have a book or a paper down as 'forthcoming' for which you now have the full publication details.

Your CV should look like a bone-china display cabinet – the best pieces should always be highlighted, your collection should be as complete as possible, and everything should be clean and shiny.

## How long should it be?

As we have said above, you will compile different CVs for different purposes. What we're going to talk about here is your 'full CV', the data bank from which you might compile shorter CVs for things like research funding applications or adapt for particular job/promotion applications.

There are many employment or re-employment agencies in many countries whose consultants specialise in helping people prepare their CVs. Their advice, and that given generally to people in non-academic public sector or commercial jobs, is that a CV should be exactly two pages long and should be accompanied by a very brief covering letter. This is the antithesis of an academic CV, which is a species all of its own. It is absolutely imperative that you understand this and resist all pressure to make your full CV the more common two-page summary. This is one of the most important things we have to tell you about academic CVs.

## Why should academic CVs be different from other CVs?

There are two key differences between academic and non-academic CVs. One is that academic CVs tend to be quite a bit longer than those of non-academics, and they get longer as a person's career develops. Between twenty and thirty pages would not be unusual for a well established professor, although someone in a much more junior post might quite rightly be expected to have only three or four pages. A second, and perhaps more fundamental, difference is that non-academics, especially when they are seeking middle management positions, are frequently encouraged to make largely unverifiable assertions about their qualities and skills rather than to list verifiable achievements. Here is an example of what we mean, taken from a website offering advice on putting together non-academic CVs.

Rather than launch into a profile or a long list of achievements, try something like this (for an office manager):

High volume and high quality process: deadlines always met; systems constantly improved; burdens lifted from senior management; expert at delivering a combination of certainty and positive client image in a multi-functional role covering admin, account tracking, document production and customer enquiries.

- Skilled and loyal team developed.
- Contribution to new IS development strategy.
- Effective use of global project management network.
- Diary, logistics and contacts for international expert teams.

(www.workthing.com/servlet/quiz?action = answers, accessed on 27 May 2002)

In contrast, academic CVs should never make vague or unsubstantiated assertions, for two reasons. First, it is an inherent part of academic life and training that we look for the verification of truth claims. Proving or justifying what we have said is part of our culture. All the claims we seek to make in our research and teaching work need to be backed up by some sort of evidence. Second, much of our work and what we achieve is done via substantial public events, for instance the winning of a research grant, the publication of papers, conference presentations and so on.

Consequently, you will not be able to include some of the work you do in your CV. For example, time spent supporting students and colleagues emotionally may constitute an important part of your working life, but is not verifiable and cannot be put into your CV. This is one reason why people who do a lot of this kind of work (most but not exclusively women) often end up with less impressive CVs. Be aware of what is and what isn't CV-able work and draw appropriate boundaries, looking after your own best interests as well as the well-being of others.

## My institution insists on its own standard CV format. Why can't I just use this for all purposes?

Many institutions feel they need to keep standardised CV-type information on their academic employees. There are legitimate reasons why they might need such information in a standardised form, for example, external research or teaching audits or validation of professional qualifications. It is vitally important to realise that the university decides what information it needs and in what format purely for its own interests. This does not necessarily mean that its requirements are unhelpful, but you can't assume that the university's interests and needs are synonymous with your own. If your university does insist on holding a CV on you in a certain format, it can be very tempting, to save yourself time, to think that it will do for all purposes. This is a false economy. If you need to save time, it would be better to keep your full CV in the best format you can and let university administrators select the information they need on you from it. If you need to submit a CV in a standard university format for promotion, it won't be too much work to pull out the relevant details from your full CV and assemble them in the required form.

## A framework for CV content

In this section, we set out what we have found to be a good, clear and comprehensive framework for an academic CV. We are going to take you through each of the headings in turn and explain what should appear under that heading and why. If you haven't already prepared a CV, or yours is not in particularly good order, you might well find it useful to read this section through once and then go back whilst sitting at your computer and start to construct your own CV using each of the headings we give.

In this section, we have tried to include all the many different kinds of work that academics do, and this may make it seem quite daunting reading. However, you do not need to achieve excellence in, or even include, every area – you can have a very strong CV that doesn't. You should not include any headings in your draft CV for which you have no content. For example, if you haven't yet published any books then having an empty section for books or monographs merely draws attention to the fact. However, where you do come to a heading under which you have no, or very little, content, you might give some thought to whether and, if so, how and when to develop this aspect of your work. For instance, if you are not on any journal editorial board, don't put this heading in your CV, but do give some thought to whether and how you might get such a position to include in future.

Our CV format has six principal sections and you should start each principal section on a new page:

(1)  Personal details.
(2)  Research and academic/professional standing.
(3)  Consultancy and public work in a professional capacity.
(4)  Teaching and examining.
(5)  Leadership and administration.
(6)  Referees.

We've defined a CV as 'the course of a life', but each section of your life – such as jobs, publications, etc. – should be narrated in reverse chronological order. Don't take any notice of people who tell you to put the oldest things you've done first and work up to the present. It's easier and kinder to the reader, who, at least in the first instance, will want to know about the current rather than the historical you. Prospective employers often ask for things to be listed in chronological order – remember that reverse chronology is still chronological.

This section should include the sort of basic personal details that you would find on most people's CVs, whether they are academics or not. The information should be given under suitable subheadings.

### Name

Use the name by which you are commonly known, in particular the name by which you are known in any publications. If you changed your family name as a result of marriage, divorce or any other reason then you should put your previous names in brackets after your current usage. Conventions for stating your family and given names vary between countries and between cultures. For instance, in anglophone countries given names precede the family name. If your names don't follow the standard format in the country where people will be reading your CV then you need to clarify which are your given names and which is your family name. If your name is difficult to pronounce in the language of your CV or is written using a different form of script (say you are Japanese, Russian or Greek writing a CV in English or vice versa), then it would be kind to readers to adopt a spelling that aids pronunciation or to give them some other indication of how to pronounce your name. Quite often people adopt names that are significantly different from their given names when moving from one language system to another. You should not feel obliged to alter your identity in this way. You want to make it relatively easy for people to use your real name but they should make an effort to do so.

### Date of birth

This may be a prickly point. Selection committees always like to know how old the candidate is, as it helps them to judge the achievements of the candidate. There is little point in leaving your age off – the fact is that readers will be able to make a pretty accurate estimation of your age if you have sent them a complete CV.

## Contact details

Prospective employers need to be able to get in touch with you in order to call you for interview or to let you know that you have (hopefully) got the job. You should include your regular postal address, telephone (work, home and mobile) numbers, fax number (if you have a confidential machine at home or at work) and email address.

## Nationality and/or work permit status

If you are using a CV to apply for a job, a prospective employer will need to know whether or not you will need a work permit to take up the post. If you are anything other than a citizen of the country where you are applying for the job, with a name that sounds as if it belongs to the dominant ethnic group, you need to make some fine judgements about how you express this. Generally, if you are a citizen of the country in which you wish to work, it is best to give your citizenship.

## Education and qualifications

Give your educational record since leaving school here. If you think that there is some aspect of your schooling that has had a particular impact on the direction and rate of your achievements, you may decide to include it. For instance, you might have been to a school for the Deaf or had your education interrupted by war or other life events. In such cases, this may be information that is important in the interpretation of your CV. Only you can decide whether such is the case or not.

Set out your further and higher education in reverse chronological order, giving the details of the institutions you attended, dates, qualifications you obtained and titles of any dissertations or theses written for research degrees. We had a discussion about whether you should include the classification of your first degree and decided that you should put it in. If your classification was good, that's fine. Equally, if your classification was poor but you are now an academic of some sort, then the chances are that your subsequent achievements more than compensate for it. If you don't put your degree classification in, then everyone will assume that it's poor and also that you've got something to be ashamed of. For the record, Jane got a first, Rebecca got an upper second and Debbie is very proud of her lower second. If the system by which your degree was classified will not be familiar to people reading your CV, then you need to offer a few words of explanation. There may be some standard conversion formula that you are familiar with for your system.

You also need to include any additional qualifications gained, for instance professional examinations that you have passed, or advanced, high-level training in, say, software design or use. Don't include your 25 m swimming certificate or your silver medal for tap-dancing (unless you're going to be a lecturer in synchronised swimming). Keep it relevant.

## Awards and distinctions

Include here any details of prizes, scholarships (including those to undertake doctoral work), fellowships to fund study leave or other special awards such as from your professional association. Don't put your school prizes in, but do include things like awards for the best paper at a major international conference (honest, they do exist in some disciplines) or the best new book or recent doctoral thesis in a discipline.

## Employment

Begin with your current employment (if any) and then list previous ones, always in reverse chronological order, of course. For each substantive post you've held, whether in academia or elsewhere, give dates, employer, the post held and – where it isn't immediately obvious – a brief description of what the job was about. If you've been promoted within the same organisation, treat each promotion as a separate employment or sub-employment, thus emphasising the fact that you've been good enough to get promoted.

Many people do not have an unbroken record of professional employment since they left school or university. They may have had career breaks to care for children or other relatives; they may have been unemployed; they may have been doing casual or other low-status jobs because they needed the money; they may have had periods of ill health which prevented them from working; they may have been in prison, working as a prostitute, a professional gambler or doing a whole host of other activities that they would really rather forget about. Problematically, a CV really needs to show a complete life picture. It is generally better to be straightforwardly open and honest about what you've been doing. This helps in the interpretation of your CV and explains an apparent lack of productivity in particular periods or overall. You need to find the most sensitive and appropriate way of giving this information. Short periods of this sort of work or activity can usually be glossed over so that they don't look like gaps on your CV. For example, if you spent three months working in a petrol station or as a bike courier following your doctorate and before you got your first academic job, nobody is really going to notice or care much and you don't have to put it in. On the other hand, if you have spent five years in jail, the gap will be readily apparent and you need to deal with it. You are likely to be asked about any unexplained career breaks in interview in any case, and it can be much less embarrassing to deal with such queries through your CV.

## Membership of professional bodies

List here the academic and non-academic professional bodies of which you are a member. Include bodies that require verification of competence and those to which you simply pay an annual membership fee. If you are on the executive or other committees of any of these organisations then you should mention it here briefly. Where an organisation requires you to pass some kind of entry test, you should include that in your 'education and qualifications' section.

Xavier's university required him to undertake training for teaching in higher education. This gave him a postgraduate certificate in higher education, which also entitled him to join the Institute of Learning and Teaching in Higher Education. The ILT was a government-promoted body designed to 'professionalise' teaching in higher education. Xavier's university automatically processed his membership and paid his first year's subscription once he had passed his course. Xavier was aware that most UK university employers were placing increasing emphasis on ILT membership for less experienced academics. However, he was opposed in principle to the ILT and its mission and certainly did not want to continue to pay the sizeable annual membership fee. Therefore, when his first year's subscription ran out, he simply did not renew it. On his CV, under 'qualifications', he included '2002 – PGCHE and membership of the ILT'.

## Competence in foreign languages

List all languages that you speak or read other than your first language, indicating your level of competence. This information may be of importance for a number of reasons. For instance, it may affect your ability to undertake research or your language competence may be useful in seeking to recruit students to the university from other countries and cultures.

## What not to include in personal details

We think that there are some personal details that really don't belong on a CV but which, surprisingly, some, often quite senior, people persist in including. Your employer does not need to know and has no legitimate interest in knowing your marital status or the number of children you've parented. Often it's senior men who include this sort of information, usually putting something like 'married for twenty five years to wife, Susan, four sons'. Whilst they may be right to be proud of their family life, statements like this read to us as unsavoury assertions of heterosexuality, a certain sort of masculinity and righteous virility. It may be offensive to some people on your interview panel and may well lead them to argue strenuously against your shortlisting. Conversely, systems that pressurise people into including this kind of information may well militate against women – spouses and children may be seen as status symbols for men but as potential distractions from work for women. You should resist all pressures to include information of this sort either in your CV or on an application form. Leaving it out will make absolutely no difference to your job opportunities, but including it may well prejudice people against you.

Other things not to include in your CV are hobbies (this always looks pathetic and immature and is not relevant to your application) and your current salary – your CV may end up being more widely circulated than you anticipated and you might not want this private stuff to be known by all and sundry. Additionally, there may be a tactical advantage in keeping this information private for as long as possible.

### Research and academic standing

This section of your CV is particularly important when seeking jobs or promotion, as well as when demonstrating your suitability for research funding. The various subsections can be arranged in an appropriate order for your particular discipline and the demands of the university system in your particular part of the world.

## Publications

We have arranged these in what we think is a fairly commonly held view of the order of importance, from the highest to the lowest status. However, this may well vary according to your own disciplinary area and your country. If your research work is subject to some form of external evaluation or audit exercise, for instance, then the presentation order of your publications should reflect the criteria of such exercises, starting with the most highly valued form.

In the examples below we have adopted a particular layout that highlights dates of publication. The advantage of laying out your publications in this way, with a hanging indent and the date on the left, is that it enables the reader quickly to gain an impression of your publication rates and patterns. If a publication is with the publishers and they have agreed to publish it, you should put 'in press' where you would ordinarily put the date. If a publication has been accepted in principle, for instance you have a contract for a book which is in progress or an article has been accepted by a journal subject only to minor revisions, then you should insert 'forthcoming' where you would usually put the date.

## Research books

These are what we call 'research monographs' in *Writing for Publication*. They are books, by one or more authors, which deal substantively with a particular area or issue that has been researched. The information that you need to include is: date of publication, the title and subtitle of the book, the name(s) of the authors, the place of publication and the publisher, the number of pages and the ISBN. These last two items are not strictly necessary, but since you generally need them in research audits of various kinds you might as well give them here, as it saves you looking them up every time you are asked for the information. The other advantage is that an ISBN shows that this is a 'proper' publication and not some in-house report in a fancy cover. The whole thing put together should look something like this:

Forthcoming: *It's So Big: A Cultural Geography of Gozo*. Standard, B., Dogstein, D. and Lush, S. Malmesbury: KNine Publications. 144 pages. ISBN 0-9999-9999-0.

2002: *Space, Time and Place in Gozitan Culture*. Dogstein, D. and Jones, F. Swindon: Roundabout Press. 189 pages. ISBN 0-0000-9999-0.

### Refereed journal articles

These are papers published in academic journals that have been subject to the usual academic refereeing process. We explain this process in some detail in *Writing for Publication*. Include: date, title of paper, author(s), journal title, volume, part and page numbers, ISSN. Again, the last item is not strictly necessary, but as with books, it is useful to put it in. Here is an example of how it might look on the page.

In press: 'Pet civilisations: urbanisation and pet ownership in the southern Mediterranean'. Dogstein, D. *Animal Geographies*. 16 (4): 22–36. ISSN 1234–1234.

### Edited books

List any edited collections where you have been one of the editors. The format for the citations should be as for research books, except that you should insert the words, 'edited by' preceding the editors' names.

### Book chapters

This section is for chapters you have written in books edited by either yourself or others. Include: date of publication, chapter title, name of chapter authors, book title, name(s) of editor(s), place of publication, publisher, page numbers and ISBN. The entry might look something like this.

1999: 'Raining cats and dogs: the over-wintering habits of transhumant pastoralists in the Mediterranean'. Dogstein, D. in *Animals and Human Geographies in the Mediterranean*. Edited by Watson, M. and Cooper, C. Garsdon: Limestone Press. Pages 12–43. ISBN 0-1111-2222-0.

## Reports

When you do research for government or other outside agencies you usually have to produce some sort of report. Quite often it will be published on the web and/or in hard copy. Such reports are an important reflection of your academic work in both research and consultancy. Include: date, title, names of authors, details of who the report was commissioned by and who published it, plus any identifying reference numbers. The entry might look something like this:

2001: 'Animal Husbandry on Comino'. Dogstein, D. Special report commissioned by the Comino Farming Commission. Research report No. 427. Mgarr: Comino Farming Commission. 27 pages.

## Other books

This is a difficult category to define, and strictly not all the books that might get listed here are research output. The sorts of things to include are: student textbooks written for the purpose (that is, not research monographs that have been adopted as if they were textbooks), professional guides, popular books about your work (that is, books like Stephen Hawking's *A Brief History of Time*) and so on. As we explain in *Writing for Publication*, this is not a category that you should seek to fill with any urgency. It attracts little academic kudos, even if the books are very useful and sell well. Books like this should be cited in the same way as research books.

## Articles in professional journals

In some, but not all, disciplines, you will be expected to disseminate your research to non-academic users. List such publications here, giving the same details as for academic journal papers.

## University working papers and published conference proceedings

Some university departments publish staff and graduate student work in their own working paper series or in-house journals. Sometimes these are internally reviewed, but this process and the level of competition will be less rigorous than for a journal.

Some conferences 'publish' conference proceedings in the sense of making the papers from the conference widely available, usually via the web. We're not talking, here, about conference papers which have subsequently been accepted for a special issue of an academic journal or as a chapter in an edited book collection. It is also important to understand the distinction between published conference proceedings in the arts, social sciences and humanities and in science subjects such as physics, chemistry and information technology. In these latter disciplines, the publication of conference proceedings is a very rigorous peer-reviewed process akin to getting a paper into a refereed journal. In the social sciences, arts and humanities published conference proceedings are almost never refereed in this way and therefore carry little status as 'publications' even if you had to submit an abstract or paper for some kind of review prior to acceptance for the conference. Accordingly, this is a section that you may well drop as you become more senior. However, when you are at the beginning of your career, this can be a useful way of indicating that you are productive and actively engaged in academic debates.

If you have a working paper to put into this section you need to include: date, title, authors, the series and any reference numbers and the number of pages. On the printed page it might look like this:

> 1998: 'Transhumant pastoralists and their animals in the south Mediterranean'. Dogstein, D. and Buster, T. Baskerville Working Papers, No. 1998/4. University of Malmesbury. 36 pages.

If you have a paper published as part of conference proceedings you need to include the usual information plus the actual dates of the conference and where it took place. Thus, it might look like this:

> 1998: 'Pastoralists and their working animals in the south Mediterranean'. Dogstein, D. Fourth International Convention on Pastoralism. Xaghra ville: University of Xaghra. 4–6 December. Can be accessed at www.xaghra.ed.go/pastoralism/dogstein.html.

## Reviews of single books

Early in your academic career you may be asked to review books for a journal. As with conference proceedings and working papers, reviews will not count for much as your career continues, but in the early days it shows that you have engaged with your disciplinary field and that more senior people take your opinion seriously and trust you to undertake these important, albeit small, tasks. Reviewing such books can also be a useful and free way to build your library, as you get to keep the copies. Reviews of single books are not refereed.

Include: the date of the publication of your review, the title and author of the book(s), journal name, volume and issue number and page number(s). Consequently, your entry will look like this:

> 1998: Review of *The Good Shepherd: masculinities and animal husbandry in Scotland* by McBiff, B. (1996). *Animal Geographies.* 10(2): 141.

## Work in progress for publication

At any point in time, you are likely to have a variety of pieces of writing that you are developing but for which you do not yet have a publisher or journal. It's important to list this work in your CV, as it gives the reader an idea of what is 'on the stocks' – work that should be coming to fruition over the next two or three years. This will give an indication of how busy you are and the sorts of directions you are moving in. However, it's important not to exaggerate.

The order in which you list these various on-going pieces of writing should be the same as that for actual publications. In other words, start with the ones that are most prestigious. It might be worthwhile giving a short abstract of items in this section and an indication both of when you expect to complete the work and of where you hope to publish it.

Books would be included in this section rather than as 'forthcoming' only if you have yet to secure a contract for publication. Book chapters would be here rather than as 'forthcoming' further up your CV only if the editor has asked you to do it but has not yet gained a contract for the book. Journal papers belong here if they are planned but not yet written, in draft but not yet submitted, have been returned to you for major revisions or have been rejected and you are completely reworking them for submission to another journal.

The details you need to give are the working title, the authors and the proposed place of publication, together with a short abstract. The entry might look like this:

> 'Of dogs and men: masculinities and pastoralism in the southern Mediterranean'. For submission to *The Journal of South Mediterranean Studies*.
>
> This paper draws on a substantive part of my completed PhD thesis. It examines the ways in which male transhumant pastoralists in the southern Mediterranean relate to their domestic working dogs. I argue that the interspecies cultural geographies of men and dogs constitute a significant element in the construction of southern Mediterranean masculinities.
>
> Due for submission during summer 2004.

## Current and proposed research projects

A research project is any discrete piece of work on which you are, or intend to be, engaged. It might be as small as a single paper or as large as you being a member of a multi-member, multi-disciplinary international team with a very substantial amount of funding. The project might be one on which you have been employed as a contract researcher. As with publications, list the most recent (or indeed the proposed) first. If you have quite a few projects, you might find it helpful to divide them between externally funded and unfunded ones, putting the funded projects first for emphasis.

Including current and proposed research projects in the your CV gives the reader a clear indication that you are actively engaged in developing your research agendas and personal intellectual project. But be careful about looking like an unrealistic dreamer – even if you have dozens of brilliant ideas and proposed projects, don't relate them all here or you will just look like someone with pipe dreams who is unlikely to deliver. It is much better if what you do here is map out your current work and a reasonable amount of future work, all of which looks achievable (with hard work) within a reasonable time scale.

The details you give here should include:

- The project title.
- A brief précis of what the project is/will be about (not more than 150 words).
- Who is or will be working on it and your own specific role.
- Who is or might fund it and if so, how much money is involved (if you have an idea at this stage).
- The time scale.
- The expected outputs.

## Completed research projects

This section is the archive of the one above on current and proposed projects. Include the same information, but obviously you will be able to speak with more certainty about the details (especially outputs, cross-referencing these to the details elsewhere in your CV) and should also give an indication as to any impact the project has had. Again, if you have a substantial number of projects, you may find it useful to distinguish between externally funded and unfunded ones, putting the funded ones first for emphasis.

## Journal editing

Academics are involved in a number of capacities in the editing of journals. These include:

- Being one of the main editors of a journal.
- Being the book review editor.
- Being on the editorial board or collective.
- Acting as guest editor on a special issue.
- Refereeing papers submitted to the journal.

Include the full details of any editorial work that you have been or are involved with. Give details of the journal, the capacity in which you have acted and when. If you have acted as guest editor of a special issue of a journal then you need to give all the usual bibliographic details.

Organise this material in appropriate sections – generally by the five main types of work undertaken, listed above. You yourself need to judge the order in which these sections come – for instance we would place being guest editor of a special issue of an internationally prestigious journal well above being one of the editors of your faculty's in-house journal. This sort of ranking should also make you reflect on where it is sensible to put your time and effort in building up your career profile.

## Book series

When you have an established reputation, you may become the editor of a series of research monographs in your field. Your responsibilities would include seeking out potential authors and titles, reading and commenting on proposals and liaison with the publisher over the shape of the eventual list. If you are lucky enough to hold one of these positions, you should give the names of any co-editors of the series, the name of the series and its publisher, together with full bibliographic details of books already published and commissioned.

## Academic collaborations

One of the things your CV needs to demonstrate is that you are an active member of a wider academic community beyond your own university. Contacts have extra kudos if they are with colleagues in other countries. These links might be one-off or on-going and are marked by activities such as:

- Working with colleagues at other institutions on research projects, organising conferences, editing books or special issues of journals and so on.
- Visiting positions in other universities. You might have spent a period of study leave at another institution or been there as an invited special guest.
- Holding an on-going honorary position at another university such as 'Visiting Professor' or 'Visiting Fellow'. These positions cost the awarding institutions almost nothing but can look very good on your CV and enhance their institutional profile. They can also afford

you quite useful privileges such as access to libraries. If you are working with someone at another institution and feel that such a position might help you, you should explore the possibilities with your friends – and, of course, remember to return the favour.

You need to include details of each collaboration. State: the individuals and organisations involved, the nature of the links, their status (funded or unfunded, one-off or on-going) and cross-reference any tangible outputs such as publications, conferences and so on.

## Research training undertaken or given

As part of your development as a researcher, you are increasingly likely to have undertaken some sort of formal training in how to do research. In some countries, this may even have amounted to a formal qualification. In other instances you may, for example, have been on a two-day training course in using SPSS, archiving techniques or textual analysis. Quite often such courses are run in-house by universities but they are also often available through disciplinary associations, funding bodies and so on. Many professional/disciplinary associations run doctoral colloquia for research students, often associated with their annual conference. All this counts as research training and should be detailed here as evidence in support of your claim to be a competent researcher.

As your career progresses, you may well shift to becoming the provider of such training for staff and doctoral students. Some people (and some institutions) become quite well known for this sort of work. If you do this kind of work, you should put all the details here on your CV. It demonstrates that you have acknowledged expertise in this area. By the time you reach this point you won't need to include research training undertaken.

## Periods of study leave obtained

Most academics have some periods of study leave during their working lives. These are periods when you are relieved of your usual teaching and administrative duties (though not, usually, of your doctoral supervision work) in order to pursue your research work unfettered. You should record any periods of study leave here, and, if they were funded by an external body, state by whom. Give the dates, a brief description of what you worked on and, if appropriate, cross-reference any outcomes.

## Seminar and conference organisation

Being involved in organising seminars, conferences, colloquia, panels or symposia for other people's conferences is something that you can and should become involved in from the start of your academic career. This is a good way of networking and getting to know people in your field (see *Building Networks*); it shows that you are an engaged academic; it demonstrates your organisation skills; and it may well provide you with the opportunity to help edit a special issue of a journal or an edited book. In your CV, you should merely list the date of the conference, its name, where and when it took place and what your role was. If there were substantive outputs such as an edited collection with which you were involved then cross-reference this to the relevant details in your CV.

## Papers given

This can encompass a broad range of events:

- Regular conference papers.
- Conferences where you are an invited keynote speaker (common in some disciplines but not others).
- Staff research seminars given at your own and other people's universities.
- Participation in workshops, colloquia and seminar series, which are often by invitation only.
- Guest lectures about your research.

You need to specify the date, paper title, author(s), event/conference name, place where it happened, capacity in which you were there (that is, were you an invited or keynote speaker or one of the regular paper presenters, a colloquium panel member, etc.), and the actual dates when it took place. Some people distinguish between international and national conferences, but this is quite a hard distinction to draw. Is it international if it's not in your own country or if it is in your own country but people from abroad have travelled to come to the conference? What's more, in some disciplines there may not be much cross-national academic traffic in this way, whereas in others it may be the norm. We think that it's better, on the whole, to allow readers of your CV to make their own judgements about the prestige or otherwise of the event. Once your list starts to get quite long, subdivide it along the following lines:

- Keynote addresses at conferences.
- Invited talks at seminars, workshops, staff research seminars, colloquia and so on.
- Guest lectures.
- Papers given that you have submitted to a conference, workshop or whatever.

### Other conferences attended

Particularly early on in your career, you might go to quite a few conferences, doctoral colloquia, etc., where you don't give a paper but you should, of course, have been an active participant all the same. These should appear in your CV at this stage because it shows that you have been learning the ropes about how such things work. As you have more papers that you have given to put on your CV, it's probably best not to clutter up your résumé with what, by this stage, won't give you any added value in job and other applications.

### Consultancy and public work in a professional capacity

This is a very disparate area of activity that will vary enormously from discipline to discipline, university to university and country to country. The types of work include:

### Acting as a consultant, paid or unpaid, in the private, public or voluntary sectors

Work here may range from undertaking a piece of paid consultancy for a local firm to doing what is essentially commissioned research for a government department or major charity. This type of work may overlap quite heavily with research activity, and, indeed, you may have undertaken the work in order to get access to particular data or resources. It might also include acting as an adviser or expert evaluator for research funding bodies in your own or another country. In short, it's any paid or unpaid work where you are valued by a body outside your institution or academic discipline as an expert. It is, then, a designator of the wider esteem in which you are held. Make sure that you cross-reference these activities to any reports and so on that may have been produced as a result and that you have listed with your publications.

## Serving on bodies that support your profession

This work involves being a member of or chairing committees or other bodies that in some way sustain an area of professional practice. For instance, you might be a nursing academic who is a member of the general nursing council or professional body for your country. Such appointments might be one-off or on-going. This type of work, especially if you are in a discipline that has a vocational/professional orientation, signals the recognition of your expertise in circles beyond the confines of your academic discipline and also demonstrates your university's commitment to contributing to the wider community.

## Serving on local, regional, state or national committees

Such service involves being a member of either a one-off committee (such as a government committee of inquiry) or of a more enduring organisation (such as a national commission that regulates corporate monopolies and mergers, broadcasting or the arts). You should include this work only if your membership is predicated on your academic expertise. Listing it here reflects your wider standing and the fact that you act as a 'good citizen'. University authorities generally welcome staff undertaking such work, as it reflects well on the institution too. Make sure that you detail any publications such as reports that arose as a result of the committee's work.

## Professional service

This is work where you perform a professional service for a non-academic organisation. You might or might not be paid for it. For instance, you may have a fractional appointment as a law professor but also work as a lawyer, the two complementing each other well. If you have such a fractional appointment, you will need to be able to demonstrate in your academic CV that you have the requisite skills, experience and standing in professional work and you will probably need a separate CV for your professional work.

For most people however, work in this category will be much more minimal. For instance, a law lecturer may help out at a community advice centre. It's often worth putting this stuff in, as it does make you look more rounded as a professional and prospective employers might like to see that you are capable of engaging usefully with non-academic organisations, from which you may learn a lot.

## Acting as a trainer and educator

In some instances, you might provide training or other guidance or help in an area of your expertise to a non-university body. For instance, you might be a finance expert who gives master classes to major banks or an education academic who helps to provide continuing professional development to schoolteachers. Such work is evidence of the 'usefulness' of your expertise and also of your engagement with wider communities.

## Contributing from your own expertise to public debates

Sometimes debates arise in the public arena to which you may contribute from your position as an academic – or you might even stimulate such debates. For instance, there has been widespread global debate about new reproductive technologies. Academics from a wide variety of disciplines have publicly contributed to such debates – moral philosophers, sociologists, medical scientists, demographers and so on. Such work can aid informed debate, can enhance the reputation of academic work as a whole and can help build individual reputations. Putting it on your CV demonstrates that you are a good academic citizen and also have intellectual credibility with the wider public. Give details of media appearances, pieces written for the popular press and significant instances in which your work has been discussed – for instance your work might be referred to in the leader of a reputable newspaper.

## Popularising your discipline or subject

Some academic disciplines seem to lend themselves to popularisation. For instance, there is a huge appetite in some countries for TV and radio programmes on history, making some historians media celebrities. What's popular changes with the wind. If you get the opportunity to do this kind of stuff, think carefully about the impact it may have on your academic career. If you are still building your reputation, be aware that such work can be very time-consuming and may not bring you many friends.

Popularisation isn't just about entertainment, making money or becoming a celebrity. You can enhance the reputation of your discipline (and many of them need it), aid public education and may well help to attract more people to study your subject. As such, it's well worth putting this work on your CV.

For each of these categories of work, give concise details of what you have done and for whom and highlight any tangible outcomes. If the outcome is in the form of a publication, give the usual bibliographic details.

## Teaching and examining

Detail your teaching and examining within higher education here. This part of your CV is usually of interest only to prospective employers and promotion panels. Unless you are applying for a research-only job, you must demonstrate that you can pull your weight in teaching. If applying for promotion in a regular academic job, you must show that you are at least competent in this area. Additionally, if you are being appointed as an examiner of some sort at another institution, it will need some of these details.

The more senior you get, the less interested appointment panels are likely to be in your teaching profile – they generally assume that you are at least 'good enough'. Conversely, if you are at the very beginning of an academic career, your teaching experience or potential can be of great interest. If you are a research student contemplating an academic career or a researcher who's never done any teaching, it is vital that you get at least some teaching experience so that you can put it on your CV. Even if the experience is minimal, stress what you have done. Having given one or two lectures to large groups is much better than never having done it at all. It follows that if you can't get sufficient teaching experience where you are a research student then you should try to find some casual teaching elsewhere.

There is a range of information that you need to convey:

- Exactly what you have taught.
- The levels you've taught at.
- The degree of responsibility that you have held (for instance, being in charge of a course).
- The range of teaching techniques that you have used.
- Any major teaching innovations you have been responsible for – such as setting up a new degree programme or developing distance-learning material.
- Your role as an examiner apart from examining on courses that you have taught. For instance, you should include acting as either the internal or external examiner for research dissertations or theses and instances where you are asked by another institution to externally moderate their assessment of students.

Bear in mind that the terminology applied to units of teaching can be extremely confusing and vary endlessly. We are going to use the term 'course' for a discrete chunk of teaching but in your country or university it might be called a 'module', a 'unit', a 'credit', a 'program' or some other term. Also, what we are calling a 'course' might be used to denote a whole degree programme. All you can do is to ensure that the meaning of whatever terms you use is clear from your CV, that you use such terms consistently and that you adopt the most prevalent terminology for the country where your CV is going to be read. Similarly, what we call 'supervisors' of postgraduate research students are commonly known as 'advisors' in the USA.

There are a number of ways of organising this material and you will have to work out which is best for you. One fairly standard way is to give the information for each institution that you have worked at. If you have supervised a lot of doctoral students and they have moved with you from one institution to another, or you have continued to supervise them after you have changed jobs, then you might like to put these in a separate category all of their own. This is how we've suggested doing it below.

### Supervision of postgraduate research students

This work really shades into your research work (or certainly should – see *Teaching and Supervision*). Research students are those working for postgraduate research degrees and students who do research dissertations as part of their taught masters degrees.

For students on postgraduate research degrees, it is a good idea to list comprehensive details of:

- Who they are.
- The title of their thesis or dissertation.
- When they started/finished.
- How they were funded.
- Whether they were full-time, part-time, located at the university or distance students.
- If they've finished, what the outcome was.
- Any other information you feel might be useful, for example when a student's funding has been tied to a major project or if you have been particularly successful in helping students to obtain funding.

If you have (had) a lot of students, it might be clearer to set it out in the form of a table. If you have (had) only a few, it's probably OK just to have two or three lines on each.

With regard to the supervision of master's dissertations, we think it's sufficient to give an indication of the years in which you've done it and the numbers involved.

### Teaching work at [your current institution] from [starting date] to present

For each level at which you've taught (doctoral, master's, undergraduate, professionals and so on) give the years in which you've taught the courses, titles, areas for which you were responsible and any other relevant information such as particularly innovative teaching approaches or course design, or published materials from the course. If this was a major core course with big student numbers, then say so, because appointments panels will often be looking for people who can be trusted with such responsibilities.

## Teaching work at [your previous institution(s)] from [starting date] to [leaving date]

Set out exactly the same details as for your current institutions, using separate subheadings for each institution.

## Examining

If you have been involved in the examination of research degrees, then you should list the year and the institutions. If you work in a cross-disciplinary way, you may find that you are asked to examine theses or dissertations in areas where the research topic is close to yours but the student is located in another discipline. In such instances, it can be good to give the broad disciplinary area of the student, as this helps to signal the strength of your cross-disciplinary appeal. If you are in the sort of system where other universities ask you to moderate their assessment standards and processes, then state here details of dates, institutions and courses or degree programmes that you were responsible for.

### Leadership and administration within higher education

This used to be the least important part of your CV, unless you were going for a senior academic and/or management position. Sadly, we suspect that in some institutions this section is beginning to gain a new importance. It is part of the reification and deification of management, of which we have spoken previously. This means that you need to pay careful attention to maximising the impact you make on paper in this section without unbalancing your actual work practices. At the same time, whilst it's easy to accumulate fancy-sounding job titles, you also need a few choice instances where you are able to highlight, 'I did [this job] and achieved these [three] things ...'

Group these tasks by institution, using the name of the university as a subheading. The information needed includes:

- Dates from and to which you had a particular role.
- The title of the role (dean, director, course leader or whatever).
- A (very) brief description of the responsibilities involved in the role, unless this is obvious from the title.
- If appropriate, a summary of your achievements in the role.

## Referees

You will not need to give referees for all uses to which your CV is put. However, you will need them for job applications and for promotion purposes. In the next chapter we talk at greater length about the choice of referees, which must be made carefully and appropriately. For the moment, it is sufficient to say that you will need to give their:

- Title.
- Name.
- Contact address, telephone and fax numbers and email address.
- The capacity in which they know you.

## And finally, a word on presentation

No-one will take you seriously if you do not take yourself seriously enough to take care over the presentation of your CV. This is, after all, the first presentation of yourself to people who may or may not offer you a job, promote you, give you a research grant and so on. The importance of good presentation may seem entirely obvious but it is surprising how many CVs are poorly presented, confusing and difficult to read. So, a few don'ts followed by a few do's.

### DON'T

- Don't handwrite your CV under any circumstances.
- Don't put your photograph on it, however gorgeous you may be.
- Don't go over the top with artistic designs, fancy paper and so on.

- Don't use coloured paper or ink – if for no other reason than that your CV may need to be photocopied.
- Don't use difficult-to-read or very small fonts.
- Don't cram everything together in an effort to minimise the number of pages, or do the opposite.
- Don't omit close proof reading in order to eradicate spelling, grammar or other errors.

## DO

- Do lay your CV out in as clear a way as you possibly can so that it is easy on the reader's eye; if necessary, get a friend who is a graphic designer or of an artistic leaning to advise you on the aesthetics.
- Do check your CV before sending it off to make sure that the pagination works and that you haven't left any hanging headings. Remember that this sort of thing can change in printing, so just checking on screen will not be sufficient.
- If you are emailing your CV to another country where the standard paper size is different (for instance from the USA to the UK), bear this in mind when you are setting up the document.
- Do ensure that you have numbered the pages.
- Do print only on one side of the page if you are sending hard copy.
- Do leave wide margins so that people can make notes as they read.
- Do be consistent in fonts, font sizes, spellings, terminology and so on.
- Do get a critical friend, who knows you and your work well, to check it over for any errors, omissions or important last minute style points.

# 5 Getting a Job, Getting Promoted

This chapter has two principal themes: getting an academic appointment and moving up the career ladder. We set out some practical steps that you can take to help you negotiate what can be a difficult and fraught process.

The appointments system we describe is fairly generic for most anglophone countries. The USA differs in some key regards and we include a special section briefly summarising that system later on. We also include a section on processes surrounding tenure in the US. That said, US readers will still benefit from reading the whole chapter.

## Be prepared

You need to be ever prepared for job and promotion applications. This is why we went into such detail on the subject of CVs and urged you to use your CV as a tool for shaping yourself up for successful job applications. In addition, you need to pay careful attention to your networks and your public reputation if you are to be successful in the job field. For instance, many senior academics sitting on appointments panels may have made a point of watching you perform at conferences or you may have caught their eye through a performance at conferences.

## Desperately seeking a (first) academic job

A number of sources of information are available for locating suitable posts to apply for.

- *Paths into academia.* People seek their first academic job from a variety of spaces and places. If you are a research student you should have access to job-finding networks via your supervisor, other mentors and department. If you enter via the professional or teaching routes, you may have established networks, or an institution seeking to employ you may proactively approach you.
- *Press advertisements.* In most countries, dedicated advertising media exist for academic jobs, usually through whatever the local equivalent of the higher education press is. Sometimes it is a supplement in a daily paper. In addition, there are often email networks on which vacant positions are advertised. Especially if you are seeking a job in another country, you will need to be dedicated to accessing the media and the electronic notifications if you want to locate posts. Most universities also have a page on their own websites advertising vacant posts. These are very useful if you know where you want to work. Some parts of the media offer email alerts for jobs and if you are serious about your job hunting you should sign up for these services. Also, ask your friends and mentors to keep an eye open for jobs that might suit you. Given the commitment of most universities to equal opportunities, and therefore widespread advertisement of most jobs, you have few excuses for missing suitable posts as they come up.
- *Personal contacts.* Some job opportunities come about only as a result of your networks of personal contacts and you need to be proactive in letting such people know that you are seriously in the job market. In some fields where it is difficult to find suitable candidates, jobs may not be filled on advertisement and may lie dormant until a suitable potential appointee comes to the attention of the department. Proactive universities, especially when it comes to research, may be willing to create posts in order to attract someone whom they really want. Whilst this is much more likely if you are more established and better known, it can happen if you are particularly outstanding or in a real shortage area. You have to make such opportunities happen by careful networking. For instance, you might engineer yourself an invitation to your target department to do a seminar, or talk diplomatically to a senior member of the department about the possibilities. Do not come over as pushy, aggressive or needy. If you are doing a research degree, ask your supervisors and mentors to spread the good word about you and your work.

Even in a situation in which jobs are openly and widely advertised, you will be in a much stronger position if you have proactively used your networks, have a solid reputation and are known to the people who will make the appointment.

## Applying yourself

Once you have found a post you want to apply for, you have to engage with some sort of formal process. First off, you need to get hold of the full job specification. This should set out the range of duties, the sort of interests, qualifications and experience the institution is looking for and, often, but not always, a reasonably detailed person specification. The latter document will set out the essential and the desirable characteristics required of the ideal candidate.

Employers are sometimes excessively optimistic about the calibre of person that they are likely to attract and pitch such specifications accordingly. When you read such documentation you have to do so with a realistic estimation of the sort of person who is actually likely to fill the post and whether you fit the bill. Research has shown that, when men read job details, they tend to convince themselves more easily that they meet all (or enough) of the 'essential' requirements and, indeed, most of the 'desirable' ones – than women do. Particularly if you are female, you should bear this in mind and talk yourself up (in your own mind and in your application) rather than down. Usually appointment panels will take the best person available on that day, provided they meet minimum standards, rather than not appoint and try again another day because their wildest dreams have not been satisfied. You may well be that best person on the day. But don't get a reputation for applying for jobs where you have about the same chance of getting it as a snowball in hell.

Once you have convinced yourself that you are a credible candidate for the job and that you want it, you need to go about the serious business of drafting and crafting your written application. In writing the documents that will constitute this application, you need to make constant tacit reference to the job details and any person specification. Don't say, 'In your specification, you said you were looking for a person who can do $x$ and I can do it.' Do say, 'I am very competent in $x$,' and then demonstrate it with verifiable evidence.

In any job specification, the institution will say what documentation it requires, how many copies and so on. In what follows, we go through what is a fairly standard bundle of requirements.

## The application form

Some institutions persist in using standard application forms, often accompanied by dire warnings that failure to fill the form in will result in your not being considered for the post. All too often, these forms are designed in a generic way, to cover all posts from the catering manager to the deputy vice-chancellor. Whilst they almost never ask for more information than is on a good academic CV, they usually fail to provide nearly enough space for important things such as publications, or completely omit other important subjects.

Our advice is to fill out your name on these forms and then write in large letters 'Please see attached CV for all further details' in each section, possibly giving the relevant page numbers of your CV. If you don't do this, and try to complete the form, the chances are it will look like a bodged dog's breakfast and you won't look very professional. Any academic worth their salt will turn to a well crafted CV with a sigh of relief and in preference to one of these usually very poorly designed forms. If you submit the form in the manner we've suggested, you will have paid lip service to the bureaucracy but not allowed that to hinder your self-presentation.

Those institutions that still use forms commonly have them down-loadable on their websites. This enables you to fill them in electronically (and therefore not hand-write them).

Accompanying any application form there may well be a separate or detachable equal opportunities monitoring form. Personnel officers should not forward these forms to anyone who is making a decision about your candidacy for the job. However, institutions like to, or are obliged to, collect such information for their own statistical purposes. These forms can cause irritation or offence to those who either object to being categorised or who don't fall neatly into the categories offered. Fill them in if you feel happy about it, but it's not compulsory.

## Your CV

We dealt extensively with your full CV in Chapter 4. Once you have decided on the job you wish to apply for, you may well need to 'tweak' your final CV to make sure that it properly and directly addresses the job details and person specification. You may need to cross-reference items in your CV with your supporting statement or letter of application (see below). In that case, ensure that these items are easy to locate.

## Covering letters and supporting statements

Some employers will ask you to make a 'supporting statement' in your application whilst others will ask for a 'covering letter'. Yet others don't specify anything. Traditions vary between countries. We can't over-estimate the importance of either a strong covering letter to accompany your application or a supporting statement. You must provide this, even if you are not directly asked for it.

In this statement or letter you shouldn't repeat what is on your CV. Rather you should weave a story around what you have and what the institution is looking for in order to oblige the reader to see you as a successful person in the job. It is essential that you respond directly to the selection criteria, job description and any person specification. You will also need to consider what the institution is like so that you can present yourself as a credible employee who will 'fit in'. It can be useful to divide your statement or letter by subheadings, either related to the person specification and the job description or, if that doesn't work, under the generic categories of research, teaching, work in a professional capacity (if relevant) and administration that will mirror the structure of your CV. You might choose to pick up on the institutional language or that used in the job details as a means of engaging the very particular audience that will read your letter.

This piece of writing needs to be cogent and precise. Take the time to find self-contained examples and/or statements of fact that concretely demonstrate your suitability for the post. As with your CV, you shouldn't make things up that can't be substantiated. However, you will need to present yourself in the best possible light – after all, this is an important part of your sales pitch for the job. Don't try to say every-thing; rather, draw the reader in and make yourself look alluring enough to secure an interview. Whilst being confident and assertive, you must avoid being boastful or exaggerating your accomplishments. Be aware of any cultural differences between you and the institution that you are applying to. For instance, what is appropriate respect and modesty in one culture can come over as cringing self-abasement in another – and vice versa.

Depending on the seniority of the job and the depth of detail of the institution's selection criteria and person specification, your letter or supporting statement should generally not be less than two sides of A4 or letter-size paper and not more than three to four sides. When it comes to very senior appointments people may submit extensive research and indeed business plans.

As with CVs, you need to take care with your use of language and presentation on the page. Use a sensible-size font that is also easy on the eye but looks crisp and professional Don't use coloured paper or ink because the pages will be photocopied. The only handwriting permissible is your signature at the bottom of the letter. Use the 'spill chick' (*sic*) function on your word processor and above all make sure that this part of your application reads well.

## Referees

You will be required to name referees who can comment on your suitability for the post. The job details will specify the number of referees and may impose special conditions, such as a reference from your current employer. The choice of referees is a serious business and may make or break your application. The panel's perceptions of the quality of your referees may influence their shortlisting decisions if you are a borderline for selection for interview. The status of your referees and what they say about you can be very influential at the interview stage, especially if it is a close call between you and someone else. An ambivalent reference can be used by a panel member to argue against you if they prefer someone else.

So what should you take into account in choosing your referees?

- Choose people who are likely to have some status with the selection panel – for instance because they know them by reputation or because they are in very senior jobs.
- If at all possible, include at least one reputable referee from another country. This will demonstrate your international standing.
- Choose people who know your work well, as they will be able to comment in authoritative detail on its quality.
- Use someone who is close to you but not too close – for instance, not a collaborator who is also known as your closest friend, lover or spouse. If you are Laurel, don't use Hardy. If you do, the reference will not be taken as seriously as it may deserve.

- Don't use people who are junior to you, or junior in relation to the job for which you are applying. Ideally, your referees should have done this type of job themselves and thus be credible commentators on your suitability.

- Generally, you should avoid using non-academic referees. Academia is a system largely predicated on peer review and collegiality, so your peers are the only people who can adequately comment on your academic capabilities, contribution and credentials. You might, exceptionally, use a non-academic referee alongside your academic ones, if applying for a job that emphasises your potential to undertake consultancy, build links with industry or deploy practitioner expertise.

- If you are a research student applying for your first job, it would be very unusual not to have your supervisor as one of your referees. Failure to do so might raise doubts in the selectors' minds. If your relationship with your supervisor is problematic, seek a resolution with them or your institution on this point at least so that you have someone suitable to name. If you have been independently examined for your research degree and your examiners were positive about your work then you might like to ask them to be referees.

- Do not fall into the trap of thinking that you have to name your head of department or dean (that is, the person to whom you are directly and immediately accountable) as a referee. You may have a problematic relationship with such a person, they may be junior to you or to the post that you are applying for. They may well have a vested interest in stopping you from leaving.

- Before finally selecting your referees, you should politely and discreetly sound them out as to whether or not they will be able to give you a positive reference. Don't use them if you are in any doubt.

Roy was a junior member of faculty in a school of social policy at a teaching-oriented university. He had a PhD and a very successful research track record as well as being an accomplished teacher who carried a large teaching load. A plum job came up at another university in the same city that would have been perfect for him. He applied and named his head of department as a referee, erroneously believing this to be essential. His head of department was on the same grade as he was but had neither a PhD nor a research record of any sort.

▶

> When his head of department received the request for a reference, she went to Roy and said that she did not feel comfortable giving him a reference because she had 'doubts' about his capacity for the job. Roy knew that his boss wasn't really in a position to judge, but by that point could do little about the situation. In the end, after many uncomfortable discussions, the head of department gave him what could be regarded as, at best, a rather ambivalent reference. Roy was interviewed but did not get the job that he was in all probability well qualified for.

When you have selected your referees, before you send your application off, always ask their permission to name them. Let them have a copy of your complete draft application and the job details so that everyone is singing from the same hymn sheet when they are talking about you. Even if they have given you blanket permission to name them for any job that you apply for, it is still courteous to let them know about particular applications and send them the relevant materials. You need to check that they will be available to respond to the employer's requests for a reference in a timely manner. It can be a good idea to indicate to your referees which aspects of your work you would like them to emphasise in their reference.

Regular and trusted referees are likely to have a sense of whether it is the right job for you and you can use them as a sounding board in this and other regards. They may give you useful feedback about the quality of your written application.

Remember that writing good references takes time and care, so be grateful and make life easy for them by sending them stuff by email so that they can cut-and-paste if they want to. Some referees may ask you for some basic text to work from – it can be quite hard to be positive about yourself but that is a bullet you have to write. It is always courteous to let your referees know the outcome of any application that you have made.

### Wrapping it up

When you have completed your forms, polished your CV, written your supporting statement or detailed letter that addresses the job criteria and secured good referees then you are ready to wrap up this stage of the process.

If you have written a supporting statement rather than a letter, you must also draft a very brief covering letter explaining that you wish to apply for the post and listing the enclosures. If, instead, you have written a detailed letter, you need to make sure that this basic stuff is included there. You can do so by opening your letter of application with words such as as: 'I would like to apply for the post of Lecturer in Archery at the University of Sherwood and enclose my CV and completed application forms. I would like to take the opportunity in this letter of explaining why I am particularly suited to this post.'

Do not include any unrequested material, especially photocopies of degree certificates, open testimonials or student evaluations of your teaching. Make sure that you send off the requisite number of copies and that you meet the deadline. Many institutions will now accept applications by email and such routes can buy you extra time. However, be aware that your carefully laid out documentation may suffer in electronic transmission, so send everything as one PDF file to avoid documents being overlooked and to preserve the formatting. If you send your application by regular mail or courier ensure that the delivery is recorded. If posting your application to another country, check out any vagaries in its postal system – you are safer using a reputable international courier service.

Do make sure that your completed application is as good as possible: people on selection committees will not believe that you can do the job properly if you can't put together a persuasive and well presented application. Sloppy applications imply sloppy people.

Once you've submitted your application all you can do is wait. University procedures vary by institution and between countries. Generally what happens is that applications are collected by the institution's personnel department and then passed to the chair of a shortlisting panel. All applications will then be considered by the people responsible for the shortlisting, usually against the published job criteria if good equal opportunities practices are being followed. Those people selected for interview will then be contacted either by letter or email. Unfortunately, few institutions bother writing to the people who are unsuccessful at the shortlisting stage. If the closing date has passed some time ago and you have heard nothing then it is probably safe to assume that you have not been shortlisted. However, don't get downhearted too soon – sometimes the work of shortlisting takes an unfathomably long time. If you are chewing your fingernails you can always ring the personnel department and ask what is going on.

## So now you've been shortlisted

The invitation to your interview should set out the details of the actual process and perhaps even who will be on the interview panel. You will be asked to confirm whether or not you will be attending the interview. If you have any special requirements that pertain to your visit, for instance of a dietary, travel or physical access nature, you need to make sure that the institution knows about them. If the date is a bad one for you because of an arranged holiday, another job interview or for religious reasons and you really can't make it, then you can try asking to be interviewed at another date. Depending on how eager they are to interview you, and other constraints, you may or may not be successful in getting a more suitable date. In the main, it's best to attend when requested if at all possible.

If you haven't yet started to publish, then, at this stage, you may be asked to submit some pieces of unpublished writing (such as a draft of your entire thesis or chapters from it). This material may be used as the basis of questioning in the interview or may simply be requested to reassure the institution that you are as far along as you have claimed to be.

## Checking things out

You will have done your homework on the university before applying for the job. An invitation to interview will give you further opportunities to check out the institution and department in more depth. It is best, if at all possible, to do this well before the date of the actual interview. You should have time when you visit for your interview to do further research – but do not let this distract you from the serious business of the interview itself. If you are concerned that you haven't or won't have sufficient opportunity to find out about the university, you should phone the head of department and work out a way of doing so. Remember that you have to choose them (almost) as much as they have to choose you, and you need to have a feel for the place where you are hoping to work for the next few years. There are a number of things you should investigate.

- If you know who will be on the interview panel, find out what their interests and reputations are. This will help you plan how you will field their questions.
- Try to pick up the atmospherics on campus. Does it feel like people are reasonably happy there or do most people seem oppressed and

miserable? Are your prospective colleagues friendly and welcoming, or are you likely to find them difficult and stand-offish?

- Visit the library to see if they take the journals you want in either paper or electronic form, and have a sufficient stock of publications in your areas of interest. If they haven't and are making this appointment to build up a new area of work, you need to ask what the prospects are of improving the situation.

- Ask to see some typical staff office accommodation or, perhaps, even the office designated for the post holder. Think very carefully about places that ask you to share an office or want to give you one that is poorly located or very, very small.

- Find out about the general levels of financial and other support for research. For instance, is there a reasonable amount of money available for going to conferences?

- Ask people at the level you would be appointed to about their teaching and administration loads. You are more likely to get an honest answer from them than from their bosses. You can also ask the same people about any onerous local work conditions, such as a requirement to spend a certain amount of time on campus.

- Does the campus feel pleasant and a personally safe space in which to spend your time? This may be particularly important if you feel vulnerable or are in the habit of working late at night or at weekends in your office. Are the facilities for eating and socialising with your colleagues good, or at least reasonable?

- If you are physically disabled, what is the access like? Will you be able to move around the campus and use the facilities?

- Unless you are going to move house anyway, check out how easy it is for you to get there from your current home. If you do have to move, then you will need to look at house prices or rent levels for suitable accommodation. Is the housing in the vicinity affordable or desirable for you?

### Social niceties

The interview process may include some organised 'informal' opportunities to meet prospective colleagues or the panel. This may vary from a buffet lunch with other members of staff to a formal bib-and-tucker dinner with the interview panel and other candidates. The usual rules apply here. Don't get drunk, spill your food, be offensive or disgrace yourself in any other way. Remember that, despite their helpfulness and informality, such occasions afford an opportunity to observe you and will be used as such.

Think very carefully about your dress and grooming for the interview. You can't go to an interview in jeans and a T-shirt (however well branded). Interview panel members usually dress smartly for the occasion, as a mark of respect for the candidates, and you should dress to reflect the seriousness of the process. That said, make sure that you are not too flashy in your clothing, feel comfortable in what you are wearing and look natural. Highly sexualised clothing has no place in an interview situation. If you sweat a lot, it's advisable not to wear a colour that will show it – white shirts and blouses are generally best. If you are menopausal and have hot flushes (flashes), make sure you are not wearing clothes in which you will feel hot. Be too cold rather than too hot. Do make sure that your general grooming, including hair and nails, is good. Unless it's part of your ethnic traditions and identity, if you sport facial piercings or wear a lot of earrings, then take sensible advice about how this is likely to be perceived. You may have to tone it down a bit for the day.

### Presenting yourself

Most institutions will ask you to make a brief presentation to your prospective colleagues, and sometimes members of the selection panel, as part of the interview process. You may be asked to give a presentation on your research or be given a specific topic such as 'What will your contribution to the teaching and research of this department be?' Yes, such questions are usually that vague and uninspiring. Although this is ostensibly a less formal part of the process, don't underestimate its importance.

- These events are designed to enable a wider group of colleagues to form a judgement about the shortlisted candidates and have some input into the selection process. There will be a mechanism for your audience to give feedback to the interview panel about your presentation.
- If you don't perform well, but you get the job anyway, those who were present may harbour suspicions that there was something defective or corrupt in your appointment. It may take a considerable time and hard work to outlive a poor reputation gained at this stage.

- This is another part of the process of letting you gauge what kind of place it is. If you are asked a series of really ridiculous, dumb questions about your research, or the people seem to have absolutely no interest in anything you say, you have to think hard about whether you really want to work in that place.

These events are nearly always (and certainly should be) run on a very tight schedule and you absolutely must stick to the time you have been given for your presentation. You should be told beforehand how long you should speak for and should also allow adequate time for questions. This means that in preparing your presentation you must rehearse, rehearse, rehearse, with a stopwatch, and get your timing perfect.

Rehearse in front of your critical friends and/or family. Get your rehearsal audience to ask you questions as well and to give you feedback on how to improve your performance. Such rehearsals will make the real thing feel a lot more familiar and comfortable and you will feel confident that you know what you are doing. On the other hand, don't overdo it such that it comes across as stale on the day.

We have serious reservations about the use of PowerPoint in most disciplines, although we understand and appreciate that in some fields it is both the norm and necessary because of the nature of the material used. Our advice is not to use PowerPoint unless it is expected and/or absolutely necessary. The technology is notoriously unreliable, and setting it up, using it and coping with failures can seriously erode the short time you have available to make an impact. If you need visual aids, overhead projector transparencies are quite adequate for most purposes, safer and more flexible. Our major concern with PowerPoint is that all too often the technology dominates the person who is presenting, and this event is all about making you shine.

Michel was called for interview for a job in an information technology-related specialism. Like the other candidates, and quite appropriately, he turned up with a PowerPoint presentation on his own laptop but had failed to check in advance whether it was compatible with the projector, which it wasn't. Consequently it took an inordinate amount of time for the technician to transfer his presentation to a disk and then to a departmental laptop. The presentation still failed to run and it later transpired that Michel's file had introduced a virus on to the

▶

▶ department's machine. Not only that, Michel had brought no back-up hard copy hand-outs or OHP transparencies, so in order to see the presentation the panel had to crowd around his small laptop. All this contributed to Michel's failure to get the job.

You might want to give the audience relevant written material, such as a brief hand-out outlining your research plans or proposed new courses. Keep these very brief and very clear, but they can be a good way of maximising your impact and the audience's recollection of you and what you said at the end of what may have been a long, boring and gruelling day.

Obviously, you will do what's asked of you in your presentation in terms of content. If you've been invited to talk about some aspect of your research, make sure that you've picked something that is likely to be of interest, is pertinent to the job you are applying for and is good. If you have been set a question, make sure you respond to it, whilst taking the opportunity to get your message over. The questions are usually so vague that they are almost a licence to say what you want within very broad parameters. Jane always says that, whatever else you do, you should have a 'killer beginning' and a 'killer ending' for your presentation. These will be the bits people remember best.

Whilst the content is important, how you come across as an individual is almost as important. You need to be very positive, enthusiastic about the place, and the audience needs to feel good about itself by the time you finish. Laughter is an amazing tonic in such situations, which are often not easy for anyone. If you can engage your audience and make them feel that they would love to have you around as a colleague, they are much more likely to give positive feedback about you to the interview panel. The converse is obviously also true.

You will be asked to leave time at the end of your presentation for questions from your audience. Respond positively and enthusiastically to what they say. This is especially important if you feel that their questions are stupid; you must nevertheless answer them in a way that is not hostile, but takes them seriously whilst not being sycophantic or patronising.

## The interview itself

The formal interview itself is the main act of the selection process. That said, a killer interview by no means guarantees you the job because there are always a multiplicity of other things in play – the internal politics, how your expertise 'fits' in the department and the quality of the competition (some of whom will also have done a perfect interview).

Here are some very straightforward points about interviews. To most of you it will seem very obvious, but it never ceases to surprise us, as members of interview panels, how often people get these things wrong.

- If you are inexperienced, get some mentors, friends or colleagues who have conducted interviews for this kind of job to give you a trial run. This will let you plan strategies and also make the real thing feel a bit more familiar.
- For the interview itself, ensure that you arrive on time, allowing for mishaps such as late trains, not being able to find the right building or room, or needing an emergency visit to the toilet (bathroom). If, despite your best endeavours and plans, you are still delayed, you need to move heaven and earth to let people know what's happened as soon as possible – it may be possible for them to reschedule interviews at the last minute. If you have a long way to travel, do so at least the day before (or even earlier if jet lag might be an issue).
- If the panel is running late, someone will probably come and let you know. At this point you should ask how late and what time your interview will be. If it's quite a while, you may want to have a little walk, go to the toilet or go for a cup of coffee. But whatever you do, ensure that you get back to the interview room five to ten minutes before the agreed time.
- If at all possible, leave your coat, large bags, hat, umbrella, laptop, suitcase and anything else that makes you look like an itinerant outside the room. Usually, institutions will have a safe place for you to leave things in. If they don't offer this, then ask. You don't want your arrival in the interview room to be marked by several minutes of you divesting yourself of all these accoutrements, and the reverse at the end.
- Take something distracting with you to read while you are waiting for the interview. You will be nervous anyway, and you do need the adrenalin that this produces to give you a bit of an edge. On the other hand, you don't want to have worked yourself up into a hyperactive, hyperventilating nervous frenzy that prevents you from performing well.
- Turn your mobile (cell) phone off before the interview, but remember to turn it on again afterwards because they might be trying to call you to offer you the job.

- Think about what to take with you into the interview. You may want a small notebook and pen to jot down points if people ask complicated questions. On the other hand, don't take in huge files, copies of books, articles, theses or certificates and suchlike. The essence of an interview is social interaction and you need to demonstrate your ability to think on your feet (so to speak) without a lot of clutter or props.
- It is an inconsiderate interview panel that does not ensure there is a glass of still water in front of you. Stick to still water – the fizzy stuff may make you burp. It looks rather gauche to pull your own bottle out of your bag, and worse still to drink from the bottle. Avoid accepting cups of tea or coffee, because they are diuretic, more complicated to drink and make you look foolish if you spill them.

There are basically two sorts of interview panels: good ones and bad ones. Good interview panels arrange everything and have a style that is designed to help you show your best side by putting you at your ease (in so far as that is possible), being respectful towards you, taking you seriously and treating all candidates equally. Bad interview panels are aggressive, hostile, carry out interviews in such a way as to try to catch you out and almost act as if you're inconveniencing them by being there. We think that the style of interview can tell you a lot about whether the place will be a good one to work in. If they can't even be considerate and polite when you've travelled and taken time off work to come and see them, your chances of them giving you good employment conditions are pretty remote. That said, there are some places, usually with very high prestige, which regard the interview as a kind of trial by ordeal and if you make it over the hot coals then you belong and may well enjoy very convivial working conditions.

Unfortunately, until you go in, you are unlikely to have a very reliable indication of what sort of interview it is going to be. Furniture arrangement and body language may be your first clues. You've got to adapt to and deal with whatever situation you find. If you have prepared well, this will be easier. We don't know anybody who performs better in a hostile interview than in a facilitative one, but some people cope better with adversity, hostility or aggression. If you do have a bad experience, you have to nurse your wounds and put it behind you. However, if you find the physical environment really difficult – you might have the sun straight in your eyes or might not be able to hear people because your hearing is impaired – then don't be afraid to ask for things to be adjusted.

The number of people on the interview panel will vary according to the practice at the institution and with the level of seniority of the post. Most panels will consist of:

- A chair, who will normally be a senior academic – for example, the vice-chancellor, a deputy or pro-vice-chancellor, a dean or a senior professor. If someone like this does not chair the panel, it may indicate that the university does not take its human resource strategy seriously, that the post is not regarded as important or that the department is sidelined. The chair's responsibility is to oversee and manage the whole process, ensuring that appropriate processes are used, especially with regard to equal opportunities, and that the final decision is consistent with institutional requirements and strategies. This person may well know very little about your particular disciplinary area.
- The head of department and one or more other prospective departmental colleagues. Their task will be to evaluate your potential contribution to the teaching, research and administration (as appropriate) of their department. They will also be making judgements about whether you will be a good colleague and someone they want to work with.
- At least one other person external to the department, who may be from a different department, faculty or even institution. Generally, for regular lecturing jobs, this person is there to make sure that there is fair play and to be a disinterested third party who can proffer advice if it is needed, especially if the panel is divided or in a stalemate situation.
- If the post is relatively senior (and in some specialist instances), it is likely that there will be an external person from another institution, who will be an expert in the field. Their responsibility will be to test and express an opinion on your expertise and standing in the area.
- In some institutions there will be a member of staff from the personnel/human resources department present. However, they will not be a formal part of the committee, even if they sit in the room. They are there to guide the chair on the nuts and bolts of things such as salaries and grades and generally act in a support capacity to the committee and the candidates.

When you come into the room, you will be shown where to sit and the chair will introduce you to the panel. You need to try to make a mental note of who is who and at least what their roles are, even if you can't remember their names. Your homework on departmental and the panel members may help you to recognise their faces.

The chair will ask you the opening question and, in good interviews at least, this is designed to put everyone at their ease. The most common opening questions are some version of 'Can you tell us a bit about yourself and why you would like this job?' Come prepared with some sort of spiel to draw on in response – you don't want to look like a silent, gaping fish. Such questions sound easy and are meant to be relaxing, but can be quite hard to reply to off the cuff. In responding, don't launch into a long speech. Rather, use this opportunity to make the panel feel that it is going to be a natural two-way conversation. Even though you are the interviewee, you can usually help to set the tone of the situation.

Following this, the chair will invite successive members of the panel to ask you questions. Best equal opportunities practice, which may not always be followed, suggests that all candidates should be asked questions about the same things. If the same generic question is asked of all candidates, it needs to be very carefully phrased. Otherwise the specific wording should be tailored to each individual candidate. Below we give some nice and not so nice examples of generic questions that we've been asked.

- *In the corner of my study at home, like most academics, I have a big pile of accumulated stuff that I've promised myself I will get back to one day, when I have time. What's in your pile? What would you want to get back to first? And why?* We think this is a really nice question because it's very friendly and engaging and invites you to be enthusiastic and strut your stuff by showing that you are full of ideas and have lots of potential. It's also open-ended.
- *If you were given complete freedom to put on any course you liked, what would it be? How would you teach it? And why?* This is a good question because it may well make you think on your feet and checks out how innovative and creative your approach to teaching is. It gives you the opportunity to say how your teaching might fit the department and the job while remaining open-ended. Such a question can give you the opportunity to enthral the panel with the idea of your working at the institution.

▶

- *Of course, like everywhere else, we expect all our staff to contribute to the 'housework' by taking on some administrative responsibilities. Can you tell us about an administrative task you've done and what you think you achieved in it?* This is a good question because it opens up the opportunity for you to show that you can do tedious administrative tasks and that you've not just paid lip service to doing them but have achieved something tangible and worth while. If what you've done to date is very limited because you are at the beginning of your academic career, you need to work around questions like this by talking about what you have done (or even did in a previous career) and explaining how you learnt to do the job and met its challenges.

On the other hand:

- *How will your research change the paradigm?* This is a truly terrible question because there is no way of judging how anyone's research will change the paradigm in advance, or even more than a decade or so after they have done, and you have to be extra-ordinarily arrogant or have an inordinate amount of self-belief to even begin to imagine that your research will have that kind of impact. Such questions are more likely to make candidates feel very small and inadequate. If you get a question like this, your best bet is to turn it round and talk about the sort of impact you hope your work will make, or what you are proud of in your research to date without claiming it will 'change the paradigm'.
- *What would you teach if you came here?* This question has two hidden dangers. First, you may be tempted to play 'guess what's in the interviewer's mind' and try to come up with an answer that is 'correct' on the basis of what is likely to be very inadequate information. The second danger is that you will opt for the weak response, 'Er, I guess I'll teach whatever you want me to.' Alternatively, you can just repeat the job specification back to them, which doesn't contribute to the information value of the interview. If you get a question like this, try to use it in a way that demonstrates your interests, your expertise and your awareness of the needs/constraints of the department. You might begin by saying something like 'What this department's really renowned for is its expertise in teaching archery. Of course, I have a lot of

experience in that area and I enjoy it. Additionally, I've been developing a course on crossbows and would welcome the opportunity to add it to your teaching portfolio.

- *Are you willing to undertake administrative work if you come here?* There are really only two answers to this question, 'Yes' or 'No'. If you answer 'No' you show yourself up as unwilling. If you answer 'Yes' you will be obligated to qualify your answer in some way, and that may be difficult to do gracefully. If you are asked such a question, a good response would be 'Of course, doing this sort of work is part and parcel of this type of post. I'm quite happy to pull my weight, but naturally what I do would have to be matched to my experience and in balance with the other things that you will want from me.'

Whatever sort of questions you get, you obviously need to be very careful in your responses.

- You need to take every question and your answer to it seriously, even if it seems really stupid.
- If you're not clear what you are being asked, request that the question is repeated or clarified. Alternatively, you could rephrase the question, checking that you have it right. It might be useful to say 'Thank you for that question. Let me unpack it ...' or 'Let me make sure I've got you right on what you're saying,' 'There's a range of ways to respond to that question, including $x$, $y$, $z$, but I'm just going to speak on the first two. Is that all right?'
- If the question is complex it's perfectly okay to buy some thinking time by saying something like 'Hmmm, that's a good question. Let me think ...' rather than rushing into a garbled and grabbled response.
- In your response it's best to maintain eye contact with the questioner, but also to intermittently include the other members of the panel. Don't just respond to the chair or the most attractive person sitting in front of you.
- Try to be as engaging and interesting as possible, creating a warm, friendly glow around the room, such that you leave the panel feeling that they have enjoyed meeting you. So it's important to smile, to make eye contact and to be generally warm and approachable in

your demeanour. If you are very nervous this may be hard to do, but an interview is a kind of performance in which you need to walk the walk and talk the talk.

- Respond to each question with specifics rather than generalities. Try to work in concrete examples of things you have done or are working on. This gives substance to your claims, whether they are about teaching, research or administration. As with the opening question, avoid rambling on interminably.

Very occasionally, the general tenor of the questioning will be such that you realise that you are faced with personal antipathy and that either you are not going to get the job or even if it were offered to you, you wouldn't want it. We are not talking here about a rogue poor interviewer who may just lack social skills and be rude and abusive by nature, or a 'tough' interview. Rather we mean sustained obnoxious and personal hostility. If you ever encounter it, you'll know what we are talking about. In such circumstances, you can't make things better for yourself but you can make things worse and make yourself feel worse by failing to act with dignity. Consider Polly's story.

Polly went for an interview for a senior post at another institution, having been headhunted by recruitment consultants. She was ambivalent about whether she really wanted the job and had a number of doubts in her mind about the university – the whole process seemed somewhat shambolic and they were unclear about exactly what the job was and what sort of person they wanted.

She was made to wait in a general student waiting area, no refreshments were offered and there was nowhere safe for her to leave her bag and coat while she was being interviewed. Although the panel was running very late, no-one told her exactly how long she would be kept waiting. When she finally got into the room she felt very unenthusiastic about the job.

The first substantive question, from an external panel member, was prefaced with the remark 'You may find this question quite robust.' He proceeded to make a long series of wholly inaccurate statements about Polly's record of publication, derogatory comments about the quality of her current institution and her work in progress and openly questioned her competence. When he had finished his

▶ offensive diatribe, Polly, having decided not to get up and walk out there and then, gathered herself together, caught the eye of the other interviewers and said, almost in a stage aside, 'Not so much robust as pugnacious.' She then proceeded to demolish his statements at length. She knew she hadn't got the job at that point, but cared only that she did not allow herself to be humiliated by such people.

At the end of the interview you will usually be offered the opportunity to ask a question or contribute further information that may not have come out in the interview. Don't produce a long list of written questions at this point, it looks awful and destroys any kind of rapport that you may have built up with the panel. If you had plenty of opportunities to check things out before the interview and have no further queries it is best to say something like 'Everybody's been really helpful and hospitable, and all my questions have been answered, so I don't think there is anything else at present – but thanks for the opportunity.' Doing this is better than asking a banal question. An alternative strategy is to have a question prepared (to which you already know the answer) that leaves a favourable impression. For instance, you might ask, 'I'm currently working up a research grant application on $x$. Would the department be happy for me to pursue it and what support would you be able to give me?' Alternatively, you might want to use the opportunity to mention any key things that you didn't get a chance to say in the interview. Don't ask, 'I've heard that this department isn't very viable, is that true?' Don't ever use this opportunity for questions to start haggling over details such as study leave, salary, job grades and so on. You might take the opportunity to briefly clarify or augment an answer that you've already given.

Finally, you may be asked whether you will accept the job if it is offered. Always say 'yes' convincingly. At the end of the interview, the chair will usually check that they have the correct contact details for you should they decide to offer you the job. You will probably be given some indication about when they will be making a decision. If not, it's okay to ask.

### Clinching the deal

If you are offered the job it is likely to be by phone in the first instance. Never, ever accept a job immediately. Rather, just thank them, indicate that you are very interested (if you are) and ask when you will be sent the formal offer with details of the salary and conditions. You should also explain that you need to speak to your mentors and family about the job.

When you receive the offer, gauge whether and by how much you can bargain them up. Remember that, in terms of salary and other conditions, you are unlikely to be in such a strong position again. They are now the ones who want and need you. This sort of haggling comes more naturally to some people than others and women tend to especially hate it – to their detriment.

In haggling, you need to sort out matters such as:

- Salary.
- Job grade.
- Periods of study leave.
- Office facilities and size.
- Computing equipment and support.
- Your starting date.
- A reduced work load if you are trying to finish your PhD or a book.
- A suitable entry strategy – what and how much you will be teaching when you arrive, what administrative task you will do, whether you will be bringing doctoral students with you and so on.

If you are not offered the job, you may want to contact the institution to ask for feedback. Often this isn't very useful – especially if there has been lots of institutional politics involved. But sometimes you may get really helpful advice about how to improve your future performance.

## Back in the USA Part 1: Getting that job

While much of what we have said is relevant to academics in the USA, there are some respects in which processes differ there. In particular, things are very different for research students looking for their first academic post. In this section we explain briefly what happens for US appointments at this level.

- The university where you are doing your research degree will keep a 'placement file' on you. This file will contain references from your advisers and other people you've worked with. You may elect whether your references are confidential or open – but they carry more weight if they are confidential (that is, you don't see them).

- First appointment jobs at US colleges and universities are advertised in the early fall (probably September) through the 'professional' (i.e. academic) association of your discipline, such as the Modern Languages Association.
- By the closing deadline, you have to submit a letter of application and a CV to your target universities.
- A 'search committee' from the department is in charge of drafting the advertisement, collating the applications and selecting the initial shortlist. They will also send for your placement file.
- About fifteen people will be interviewed at the association's annual conference by two or three members of the search committee. These interviews take place in the conference hotels and last about half an hour. They will normally be about your research.
- From these preliminary interviews, three or four candidates will be invited to visit the campus – with all expenses paid. You will spend two or three days at the campus, during which time you will have a tour of the neighbourhood, informal meals and meetings with members of the department and make a presentation to the department. You will also be formally interviewed by the full search committee, who will be joined by colleagues from other departments. You will have a private meeting with the head of department to inform you about salary levels and fringe benefits, but this is not the place for negotiation. In some teaching-oriented schools, you may be asked to teach a 'demonstration class' to students. This can be very daunting and difficult, as you don't know the students or context, but you just have to do the best you can.
- If you are successful, you will be offered the job within about a week of your campus visit. At this point, you will be able to negotiate about issues such as salary and work load.
- The usual starting date for new appointments is the following September.

## Promoting yourself, getting promoted

Promotion brings with it a higher salary and more status and recognition. If you want to get promoted, you have to familiarise yourself with your local conditions very early on in the process and plan your campaign accordingly. Because the job descriptions for academics are so vague, it can be really hard to know what the expected standards are. This lack of specificity is also, unfortunately, sometimes used as an inappropriate means of punishing or rewarding certain people.

Within the requirements of your own institution's systems and processes, you need to assemble your application for promotion with the same care, cunning, networking and precision that you would attach to applying for a job elsewhere. Depending on your own institution's requirements, this can be very time-consuming. For some reason, universities often fail to put a money value on how much their own procedures cost them. In particular, you will need to present your CV, and it needs to be shaped to meet the criteria applicable. We dealt with CVs extensively in Chapter 4. You will also need to propose referees, and we dealt with this subject earlier in this chapter.

There are usually fixed cycles for promotions and these can often take an inordinate amount of time. Once your application is in, you just have to get on with your work as usual. However, if the process takes a long time and your CV changes in important ways during this period – for instance, you have a paper accepted in a prestigious journal or get your doctorate – you should write to the secretary to the promotions committee giving the additional details and requesting confirmation that they will be put before the committee.

The only time when you might buck the trend of cumbersome and lengthy procedures is if you are offered a promoted or better-paid post at another institution. If you would rather stay put, you can use this job offer as a bargaining chip to quickly get a promotion or a pay rise. This is by no means guaranteed, however, and universities often get into a situation in which they allow extremely valuable people to walk – but it's worth a try.

Given the resource constraints of most universities, the number of people who can be promoted at any one time may be significantly less than the number of people who actually merit it. This can be particularly frustrating if you are consistently deemed promotable but fall just short of this resource-determined threshold. You need to remember two things.

- Very few universities have formal processes in place to regularly review staff progress specifically in order to determine whether or not a person should be promoted. This means that you have to be proactive if you wish to pursue promotion.
- In most institutions it is significantly more difficult to advance a grade internally than it is to get a promoted post elsewhere. This is,

at least in part, because while evaluations of external applicants involve their entire CVs, internal applicants are assessed on the progress they have made since their last promotion. This can be particularly problematic if you are already over-qualified by the time you are applying for promotion – you will have a lot further to travel to your next promotion because of the benchmark that has been set.

If you don't get promoted, you should ask for detailed feedback about the reasons. Get this in writing from someone in authority if at all possible. If the feedback was verbal, then write, politely setting out what you understand them to have said and asking for their confirmation that you have got it right. Don't make any such letter confrontational or angry, however upset you are. You will be applying for promotion again and you don't want people in authority to think that you are an awkward customer.

Once you have got your feedback in writing, you need to identify specifically what it is you need to do to meet the shortcomings identified by the promotions committee. If necessary, go to see your head of department or dean and ask for the kind of work that you need to get on your CV. Once you feel that you have adequately met the criticisms of the promotions committee, apply again, subtly highlighting the changes you have made in your profile. If you approach promotion in this way, you will make it very difficult for the committee to reject you a second time. We can't guarantee success using this method, but it's the best non-adversarial one that we've come across.

## Back in the USA Part 2: Getting tenure

It is generally the aim of early career academics in the US to get a tenured (that is, a permanent) post in a university. Although everyone who teaches in a university is given the courtesy title of 'professor', the career structure begins with temporary appointment to an adjunct (or sometimes assistant professor) position. This may be full or part-time and it may be on a fixed-term contract or on a contract known as 'tenure track'. The tenure-track posts are the most sought after, as they offer some promise of permanence in the future. The scale goes up from adjunct to assistant professor (which is the equivalent of a lecturer in the UK, Australia and South Africa), then to associate professor (like the UK senior lecturer or reader; Australia and South Africa use the same term) and finally to full professor (the equivalent of professor elsewhere). However, some people who, perhaps, have a parallel career in, say, the law continue to hold an adjunct post at a university where they teach part-time throughout their career.

The early temporary positions are usually for three years at a time. At the end of the first three years of a tenure-track position, a senior member of faculty or, possibly, a committee will review your work. This review will consider your teaching, possibly including some observation of your classes, and of your research publications. On the basis of this review you will be given advice about how you are getting on and what you need to do in the next three years. Generally, this will lead to another three-year contract, although sometimes it does not happen – generally if your work is very unsatisfactory or if the university is in the process of making budgetary cuts.

Your position will come up for tenure during the sixth year of your employment and this will be considered by a series of tenure committees at different levels: departmental, college/faculty/school and university. You will need to submit supporting documentation for consideration by these committees, including:

- A full résumé (CV).
- A supporting statement making your case for tenure.
- A list of external referees for your work (though sometimes you may not be asked for this as the department will make its own recommendations concerning outside expert advice).
- Samples of your work as a researcher and, possibly, as a teacher.

If your application is successful at departmental and faculty level, consideration by the university committee is generally simply a matter of rubber-stamping the recommendation to give you tenure. If you are successful in gaining tenure, you have a good chance of being promoted to associate professor at the same time.

If your application for tenure is turned down, the university will usually give you a 'terminal appointment' for one year, which will not be renewed but will give you time to look for another job.

The advice we have given in this chapter about getting promotion in other countries applies equally to gaining tenure and promotion in the US – the differences are not as great as they appear on the surface.

# 6 Balancing Acts: between Work and Life

In this chapter we try to convince you to have a life outside work. This is one instance in which we are not writing from the basis of our own personal expertise and experience. All three of us are hopeless workaholics with a poor work–life balance. However, as Jane said in introducing herself at the beginning of the book, we would like to help the next generation of academics to be differently pleasured. So do as we say, not as we do.

## What do we mean, 'work–life balance'?

This much used phrase is a euphemism for something much more simple and straightforward: how much time you spend working or not working and how the quality of your non-working time is affected by your work practices.

People with a poor work–life balance (that is, people who work too hard and for too long) end up with broken relationships, disrupted family lives, physical and mental health problems and poor quality of life. No job is worth this. Research in the UK and elsewhere indicates that academics are much more likely to become seriously ill with workplace stress than a whole range of supposedly more stressful professional occupations. We are sure that this pattern would be replicated in many, if not all, countries in the world. The same group of workers are also renowned for the punishing length of their working week.

Don't think you are immune from all this. Take positive steps now to redress the balance in your life and keep it that way.

## Why do academics work too long?

Academic work has a number of inherent characteristics that produce a tendency to excessive and prolonged periods of intensive labour. First, the work itself and the standard that is expected are generally very poorly defined. When combined with a culture of competitive critique, this means that enough is never enough. Second, much academic work is subject to what Jane has called 'discourses of derision' in another context. That is, especially outside the 'hard' sciences, academic work can all too often be seen as of little or no value in a system where increasing emphasis is placed on the production of 'useful' knowledge. This derision often finds fertile ground among academics themselves, who either suffer from low self-esteem combined with compulsive over-achievement, or find it hard to see why anyone should pay them a salary to pursue the things they're interested in (or both). Third, academic work is frequently invisible, and tangible outputs such as publications give little indication of the actual value of the labour taken to produce them. Together, these characteristics serve to create a view of academic work, frequently internalised by academics themselves, that casts it as self-indulgent, useless and marked by long periods of time-wasting inactivity.

This poor understanding and perception of much academic work means that there is very little defence against pressure to do more and more and more and to do it better and quicker. When people protest or fall ill, the institutional response is all too frequently to place the problem firmly at the door of the individual. Thus people who cannot cope are deemed to be poor self-managers or time managers. University systems are marked by an abject lack of reflexivity in this regard.

## Discourses of time management

We have already indicated the first discourse of time management and the one most often deployed against academics and, unfortunately, inhabited by them. This is the discourse of wasted time, poor self-organisation and lack of professionalism. In this discourse, academics are useless wastrels who simply don't know what a hard day's work is and spend way too much time doing nothing or watching daytime television. If you are not managing to keep up with your work, then it's entirely down to you and your inadequacies.

The second discourse of time management, and one that we would like to promote and inhabit, is one in which time is recognised as being in short supply but in which we can take a certain degree of control and do something to ameliorate things.

There is a really fine line between these two discourses and it's treacherously easy to slip from one into the other in the twinkling of an eye. There is also a fine line between occupying the second discourse in a positive way and it being a way of not participating or being a good colleague. If you slip into the latter position, the second discourse can easily become an expression of bitter, negative sentiments and resentments. You need to understand that care and regard for yourself is not necessarily negative selfishness. Most people struggle with these balances and virtually none of us gets them right all the time.

We offer below some final handy hints (to ourselves as well as to you) on having a good work–life balance and staying sane. It is our New Year's Resolution to follow all of them, and, if we don't manage it, not to criticise ourselves too much for our failures.

## Handy hints for maintaining a good work–life balance

1. Build work-free space and activities into your daily routines. These can range from going for a nice walk with your dog, having dinner with your partner, going to the gym or the swimming pool, spending time in your garden, reading a newspaper or a novel, playing computer games or whatever pleases and relaxes you. Don't ever be guilt-tripped into thinking that you can do such things only as rewards or treats for having done your work.

2. Place strict limits on your periods of work. You may have to relax them from time to time in order to meet important deadlines, but in the main you should keep to them and take time off in lieu if you break them. Always try to have at least one work-free day during a normal working week and preferably two. Remember, even God rested on the seventh day.

3. Most academics do at least some of their work at home. Whilst this can be quite nice it can also make it quite difficult to switch off from work activities. If you have the space, make sure that your work-at-home activities are confined to a comfortable and discrete space. About the last thing you need is your computer winking at you as

you try to sleep, eat your dinner or watch television. If you can't afford this luxury then at least try to put your work away, cover your computer up and get on with the rest of your life at the end of your working day/week.

4.  Try to organise your working time so that you can use it as efficiently as possible. For instance, make time for complex, demanding tasks in joined-up chunks rather than odd little bits. That way, you have more chance of achieving something and feeling able to have your day(s) of rest.

5.  Given the impossibility of academic work-loads and your new resolve to have a good work–life balance, there will inevitably be things at work that you will simply not have time to do. You should be the person who decides what you are going to do and what you are going to leave undone. Your decision should be based solely on your professional judgement about what you need to do to be a good researcher and a good teacher. If you have to make the choice between completing an important research paper or filling in a form that will simply be filed and forgotten, it is obvious to us, and hopefully to you, which choice you should make.

6.  When you are working, don't work so hard that you are left too exhausted and depleted to enjoy your non-working time. In the same vein, make sure that your working space (at home and in your office) is safe. Do not put up with non-ergonomic furniture that is likely to compromise your health in any way. It's no good having a good work–life balance if work has left you too unwell to enjoy the rest of your life.

7.  Use at least some of your non-working time in a productive, enjoyable and creative way to look after yourself and your health. For instance, being an academic can be a very sedentary occupation, so getting a moderate amount of exercise can be an important and profitable way of spending your leisure time. But don't let this become a punishment either. If you are someone who needs time just to veg out, then take it.

8.  We think that getting away from everything from time to time is a wonderful therapy. Do take proper holidays, even if it's just visiting friends and family rather than more expensive trips. Do not take your work with you. If necessary, get someone else to check your suitcase before you leave, if you are completely untrustworthy in

that regard. A complete break, even if it is short, is likely to be much more therapeutic than simply slacking off for a few days.

9. You need to enlist the support of your friends, family and partner in achieving a good work–life balance. Debbie often initially resents it when her partner insists that she has a day off from work. By the end of the day, however, she is grateful for this stiffening of her resolve. It's often the case that academics have other academics as partners and/or friends – after all, who else would put up with you? In one sense this can be quite helpful, as you have people around you who understand precisely what the pressures of your job are. In another sense, it can be quite problematic if you collude together to maintain a poor work–life balance. Whoever or whatever your friends/family are, you need to resolve how you will manage this issue.

## And finally …

This book has been about the various elements of an academic career, how you get the right mix of activities for you, get the jobs you want and how you can balance your work with the rest of life. Throughout, we have emphasised that, although you are part of a massive globalised system, you do have agency over your life and work and can make real choices.

Anne Gold, an academic at the University of London, has devised an exercise for academics designed to help them balance all the aspects of their work and the rest of their life. We think it might be good for you to do an adapted version of her exercise on your own or with friends. You'll need a very large sheet of paper (flip-chart paper is good) and some coloured pens.

Draw a series of buckets. Four of them should be labelled 'research', 'teaching', 'administration' and 'consultancy and practitioner work' in turn. These are your work buckets. In addition, draw the other buckets that best represent your desired life outside work. These might be labelled 'family responsibilities', 'leisure', 'friends', 'relationships', 'health', 'personal and household care and management' and so on. You decide.

In each of the buckets, draw a contents level indicating how full it is – anything from empty to overflowing. Then sit and think about whether you're happy with this distribution and what redistributions are both desirable to, and achievable for you. Address each bucket in turn, consider whether its contents are appropriate and think about strategies for emptying it or filling it up. That is, how are you going to redistribute your energies and efforts? It may be that the total volume of stuff in your buckets is too great. If so, draw one final extra-large bucket to put your unwanted surplus in. Label it the 'phucket bucket'.

# Further Reading

Blaxter, L., Hughes, C. and Tight, M. (1998) *The Academic Career Handbook*, Buckingham: Open University Press. This book argues that teaching, researching, writing, networking and managing are the five key activities of the academic. Like *Moving on in your Career* this book bases its suggestions on current trends in academia towards highly competitive contract work. Although the authors state that this is a book primarily for a UK readership, the advice and research on networks are applicable across a range of contexts. This is a well researched book with extensive annotated bibliographies on academic careers and related areas. It is rather let down by the production, with a difficult-to-read style of print and unattractive layout, but is worth persisting with despite this disadvantage.

Frost, P.J. (ed.) (1996) *Rhythms of Academic Life*, Thousand Oaks CA: Sage. Peter Frost is a well known Northern American academic in the field of organisational studies. In this rather large volume he has collated the self-narrated life stories of a large number of academics. The contributors come from a fairly narrow range of disciplines, principally in the management sciences. That said, the real voices expressed here can make fascinating reading – this is the ultimate book of vignettes. If you are looking for a simple 'how to' book, this is not for you. Nor will you necessarily find upbeat narratives about how wonderful things are. You may have too much grief in your own career already ...

Goldsmith, J.A., Komlos, A. and Schine Gold, P. (2001) *The Chicago Guide to your Academic Career,* Chicago: University of Chicago Press. With the imprimatur of a prestigious US university, this ambitious book is the US equivalent of Blaxter et al. It attempts to be very broad-spectrum in its reader appeal. The authors adopt the genre of a written 'conversation' between them: they pose themselves a series of questions then provide their own answers. This can make tedious reading and perhaps the format is a little 'lazy'. This single volume aims to cover almost everything from starting a research career as a student to getting a first job, managing teaching and research and dealing with a whole load of personal issues, such as a dual-career marriages. (The distances between universities in north America mean that it can be quite common to offer jobs to partners.) Some reviewers disliked certain aspects of the way in which gender issues are dealt with – sometimes almost as an afterthought.

Lai, L. and Graham, B. (2000) *Moving on in your Career*, London: RoutledgeFalmer. *Moving on in your Career* argues that in the context of the ever-growing number of contract research staff compared with a diminishing number of permanent staff, early career researchers need to be flexible in their career plans and pay close attention to networking. The book shows researchers what is required to advance their career in academic research or lecturing and gives advice on taking alternative career paths. The book is aimed both at early career researchers and at postgraduate students. It also provides practical exercises and ideas to enhance essential job-search and self-presentation skills. The book uses engaging first-person narratives about academic life that emphasise the need to increase the researchers' visibility through collaboration, volunteering and conference attendance. All these activities can be thought of as forms of networking essential to career advancement in a competitive environment.

Sadler, D.R. (1999) *Managing your Academic Career: Strategies for Success*, St Leonards NSW: Allen & Unwin. This book aims to assist early career academics to plan and manage the main tasks of academic life. The book is written in the form of letters to hypothetical early-career academics, and as such locates its advice in the personal experience of the author, rather than an assessment of scholarly work done in this area. The book covers a broad range of strategies for early-career academics, including time management, confronting bias, choosing referees, teaching and publishing. Establishing a personal academic network, through, for example, conference attendance, the academic is forced to articulate their work over a range of contexts, and this process can be highly valuable for the researcher.

# Index